David Shapiro

NEW
AND
SELECTED
POEMS

(1965–2006)

OTHER BOOKS BY DAVID SHAPIRO

POETRY

January
Poems from Deal
A Man Holding an Acoustic Panel
The Page-turner
Lateness
To An Idea
House (Blown Apart)
After a Lost Original
A Burning Interior

CRITICISM

An Introduction to John Ashbery's Poetry
Jim Dine: Painting What One Is
Jasper Johns: Drawings
Mondrian: Flowers

ALSO

An Anthology of New York Poets (with R. Padgett)
The Selected Poems of Jacques Dupin (with P. Auster)
The Writings of Robert and Sonia Delaunay (with Arthur A. Cohen)
Alfred Leslie: The Killing Cycle (with J. Stein)
The Eight Names of Picasso by Rafael Alberti (with G. Berns)
The Collapse of Time (with J. Hejduk)
The Body of Prayer (with Jacques Derrida and Michal Govrin)
Uncontrollable Beauty (with B. Beckley)

David Shapiro

NEW
AND
SELECTED
POEMS

(1965–2006)

THE OVERLOOK PRESS
Woodstock & New York

First published in the United States in 2007 by
The Overlook Press, Peter Mayer Publishers, Inc.
Woodstock & New York

WOODSTOCK:
One Overlook Drive
Woodstock, NY 12498
www.overlookpress.com
[for individual orders, bulk and special sales, contact our Woodstock office]

NEW YORK:
141 Wooster Street
New York, NY 10012

Cataloging-in-Publication Data is available from the Library of Congress

Book design and type formatting by Bernard Schleifer
Manufactured in the United States of America
ISBN-13 978-1-58567-877-8
1 3 5 7 9 8 6 4 2

To Jasper Johns

Acknowledgments

My thanks are due first to Thornton Davidson for his extraordinary support, to David Haxton for generously letter his art be reproduced on the jacket of this book, to the many editors and poes—too many to name here—for publishing these poems in small magazines, to my first publisher Arthur Cohen at Holt, to my publisher Peter Mayer, and the entire staff at The Overlook Press for their commitment to my poetry, to my many friends and teachers that have been so important to the writing of these poems, and lastly to my wife Lindsay and son Daniel.

Contents

JANUARY
(1965)

Canticle

1

I was on a white coast once.
My father was with me on his head.
I said:
Father, father, I can't fall down.
I was born for the sun and the moon.

I looked at the clouds
and all the clouds were mounting.
My friends made a blue ring.
O we hung down with the birds.

2

I loved the snow
when the summer ran away.
Once I said:

Cricket, cricket, aren't you afraid
that you're really too loud?
He said:

David,
I don't think so.

3

Monstrous night!

I want light now! now!
I want those great stars again!
I want to know
why I keep asking my father
what he's doing on that shore.
What is he doing, anyway?
Why isn't he over here?

I saw the Red Bird too.
But where's its Wing?

I want to tell my father what I saw:
That Bird is full of fear.

The Pirates

If the pirates unleash the disastrous contractor
and all the other bonds are broken
If the freckled man like a scarlet shark
Jesus
Attacks and dies like a dot in the dark
will one dog bark for me on this bus?
Unlikely, but snow grows on the garage, and worse:
Truth is forgotten and we ants are shaken.

And all the time we have never loved more
Jealousy that inevitably reflects on us:
Doves that were left drowsing on the shore.

From Travel

Look, wind, I have run out of motion.
The four animals who wanted me now refuse
to have me, now that they have caught me,
and I seemed so desirable when I was running away.
The city limits are a kind of new dream for me.
I used to think a few blocks meant the country.

The sun was always rising behind me.
I thought the third bridge meant
I had finally escaped everything I wanted to.
Each time I was tired, I fell asleep
and, now, in this house, in this house
no one is tired and no one falls asleep.

Once I thought a car was following me,
I heard a strange language spoken in the front seat,
I was so frightened I nearly fell asleep,
but it was only another man coming up the road
whispering something to me I couldn't understand;
half the way over the hill I started laughing at him.

Don't mock me for not controlling myself,
my first problem was getting enough food,
and then I could think of what country I was going to.
My old gold clock kept giving up,
the only time I knew was dark and light
and hunger time; all of the time I was tired.

Now the whole side of the house is white,
once it was the color of crushable plants,
once it was the color of weeds bending back,
once it was the color of the egg of a snail,
once it was the color of the top of the tree,
it was never the right color for you or me.

I took a long look at what you did yesterday
for me, and I report thank you from my friend.
It's too late to sit down in the backyard in the snow
and watch it come down, it's too late to eat the snow
like last year or the night before you came
Before you came? what could I have done then??

Two Poems on the Emotions

1 Dust
They commune at 7:30 where I walked my arid hands
This woman, she forces me to notice bloody lambs
While she selfishly contrives to the word is arouse me on the snow-dunes
you realize in a few moments she is going to smash it

Other small people scrawl in their journals about vacations
They escape thinking lust is a withered thing
Whereas on one hand I have the withering complex
they get excited by dismembered chickens and dance up and down

2 Love
As on the Greek island of Corfu, at sunup,
we saw the dying woman posing nude for the
kittenish photographer who was, for example,
her own father—it demolishes desolation
it makes one feel in the company of erections
or the stiffer tenderness of green jade or
the glossy tenderness of blue marble
No longer in the realm of "personal feelings" but
Beauty, as in Keats—Only the word exists for
ten thousand Roman soldiers slaughtered at Cannae
this involves much light in the mystery while
Juliet has her hand on my door

The Will

1

I know the party of the sun
The sun dirigent and wealthy over the hair
The sun of round cancer on the gray breasts of the sky

and I understand that the commitment of the intellect is pitiful
even in the stage of the lapse of mind, where the speech is senseless
and the jaw kind and calm as a child's mouth.

Then fathers moping in the stove of the sun
grieve all their school and tears of a will
that drove them so, the intellect and changes of the Sun.

But when the jaw falls, and the stars are perfect depressions
in the sky thru which the wind dwindles and thru the stiff oak branches
I can see the advantage of literature to the mind.

And, at last, I become serious, in this room, with a smile.
And the directions of the wind and sun outside this room
remind me

of where the brown fields, in the wind, and the park
become silent; and I notice also, distinctly and quietly, in this room,
the insinuations of men turning to their wives in the descending cars.

2

That fit of one heart is a predicament. But what arrives, what
arrives like the monk of the flesh? Who is that gaping guest
rules in the kingless blood and makes us men?
I hear the paltry wind bang at the homely boughs

and the highways of men turn to their wives under the moon.
What rings the sky in the cloud, what drives the sea?
What visible hero and what dark face of this woman
who takes her hands from her cheeks and holds the infant up

to tears, in the night, as the ragged boys congratulate and borrow
from the heart of the lady holding the infant in her wellbeing
and the screams of the infant born again and again
in the dark to every citizen of a name.

3

When shall we wake to the recession of dreams?
Is it to wish the rose the profit of the loam
or the August star the ethic of the sky?
Tonight the children wish they had made friends.

And those weapons which separate us from the sun
and from each other, the will shall keep
from all imagining,
born of an outburst and cudgeling light.

So that all who survive the mind of a man are
wealthy men, who are defended and understood;
and those who grip an hour of blood within their hands
—and die of Silence in the year of reasonable men.

(1961)

Zuzu at the Circus

The dancers are coming! The pale green horses
The Prince, those flashing teeth, and now the circus!
I take Zuzu to lead him through the courses
Oh but I've gripped him too hard and some pus
Oozes from a blister in his left paw.
Well, well. I have to end my letter, darling.
It's February in the Book of Law
And it's too hot in the radiator to sing.
But all that spring the dancers kept on floating
In with drum-kettles and with dangerous legs
Slim white legs which the girls whispered something
About—which then turns middleaged and sags
    But not the circus or the pale green horses
    The world is energy—nobody forces

January

I want you
This morning is
winter rocking
my ear: there is no
promise for it,
but simultaneous
and soft voices
deprive, deprive
No stain
is on the streetlight
between falling things
and the hands only
wave dusty loaves
as the heart in
her cone of cold
waves the winter witch
on all the boys
making them wake and twitch
I want you
your hair and the puzzling
things your body
removes   Is it winter
The school is
Thirty girls are running
laughing to watch
the teacher strain
I cannot listen anymore
because I want you
because there is no name
that morning recreates
except yours
because my feeling
surrounds me
I want you

Poem

for Berele Chagy, Cantor, died 1954

I wouldn't poke my head
through time or the gramophone
to see my grandfather's face
so fleshed with smiles.

Today my sister sinks in a pile
of toys in front of the speaker,
his record on. Her white fists
knock at it softly, as he dies.

20 / David Shapiro

Canticle

1

In winter I ran under the streets.
I sank by the seashore under the dead hotels.
All the gulls crept down in the dirt,
even the moon crept down in that ditch,
O the moon was with me once.

Father, what does the rock
say about it now.
What is the rock doing
in the whirlwind.
Father, father, you are on fire.

2

Look. The cold squirrel sang on the shore.
I said: I am going to be a blue man, father.
All the blue men are on fire.

He said: Look. Everything about the grasshopper
is strange.
O he had one guitar.

3

But how did the spiders
get out of the ditches
and how did the men
come out of the houses
at the end of the winter
into the soft night.

And what about the sound
it made on the coastline
of those great birds,
what about the hooks
the whirlwind has
for those white flukes
the ghosts inside those
great birds the gulls
calling all the men down.

Who said: Sick eye, get out of the way of the wind
He is on fire

    4
Paul, be rich
Be rich, Paul
All the sick men of the World
are the kings of the World
and I have seen
crowns in the whirlwind for them
and I have seen
crowns on their heads.

The sea gulls are on the water, Paul.
They are going crazy
trying to wash off their spooks.

                Bird, bird, make them sleep.

What are they killing
the sick men for,
Paul, what are they killing
the sick men for
They are really on fire
They never stop killing
the men who speak clearly
and, now, that is a flaw
and that is an error
and that is an error, Paul,
and that is an error
called Death, Death.

Recalling Palace Grounds

Dear friend

Something is stirring behind your face.

How long have I known you, so beautiful,
& not told you about it

Dawn has brought the ships out. Dawn
keeps breaking our ships.

It's morning.

Can I tie your hair again?

Deal Winter Composition

dry tongues
       might;
and a slogan
       that nurtures
the sea bird and the
       loser
it shall
       console them
All the gray
       squadrons
of mental
       concretion
the endless
       traffic and
surrender
       of poet
and tendril,
       all the melancholy
congregation
       tracts and domains, expansions,
overheard, or
       partly heard even

it shall
       console them:
a face a glyph
       climbing in the mist
toward you,
       and a long granitic coast

stretched before your thumb your
       eyes, gestures
and groves,
       in a white season.

Other Flowers

1

I had a gold ring once.
I had the shadow of a cloud.
O I had other flowers once.

I had the station where I met my father, leaping.
I had a dream about a great bridge.
I lived in a lonely booth.

I had the ocean and the green blood of the algae.
I had the filthy seagulls in a circle on the sea.
I had one of those tunnels in the sand.

I had the rain coming and the sun—
I had to leave because it was always dark in those tunnels.
I had my fingers in the waves.

My sister the honeysuckle made me sleep.

2

It was always late afternoon on the beach.
and I remember the eye of a fish
that never closed.

on the white boards at Deal
and all the gulls that put it down
with a wild sound on the shore.

Really, I thought that fish could cry.
and now I wait for the next note
Lord I wait

for this terrible thing
that is coming in the wind
to ruin my side of the house.

3

Mother, the grapes are growing.
The tendrils cling even if they don't grow.

Look how fast you lost your father.
Look how dark his room was.

I'm so cold I'm sick.
I'm sick of the snow.

Father, father,
this year I shall be gentle to my good friends.

I saw a white bird settle when you called.
My mind settled on the white bird.

I said:
Come closer, bird.

First Love

I imagine you dressed up as a gowned Hasid
A blackbearded girl—a girl I might have married
A stick we take to bed and call John in bed
Later a white-breasted Protestant girl to be buried.
Who are you and what cruelty in what theater
Do you still play cello and strip for friends
Atlantic City fingers warmed by the electric-heater
Sun—a decadent image everybody understands.

And you smile by the chorus of a Psalm of David
Your smile twirls in the air just before I cry
"Your team is my team" and you change the bid
On your body to a strangulating price I cannot buy.
Slowly walking in Boston with a music note
Your composition stabs me like a bat.

Giants

Giants are much too beautiful
They live in a house called bigger dimensions
They never suffer from delusions of grandeur
and I have met many giants and this is always true
A giant will always pity you

Still, giants sleep with their eyes on their business
which mainly now is the killing of tourists
the flow is getting smaller since the end of the summer
the fall of leaves keeps many customers away
still, I could never say goodbye
to all my friends among the giants
and they have frightened all my enemies away.

The giants know that I'll be strong some day
for I have planned one insuperable attack
against this habit of closing my eyes when I sleep
because I want to hold on to light as long as I can
and because I want to kiss the small of your back.

Five Songs

With Debra

1 The King of the Elephants
We won't favor you
For supper
We won't call you in
To eat lunch

But we love you
Come when we don't call
You have white pearls
And blue stones

2 We Are Ugly
You don't know my sister
She has white teeth
I commend her
You don't know my sister
Who is named the purple pearl

She goes under a bridge and gets lost
She doesn't come home till she dies

3 Now About God
God is help
And his name is softer too
Than the arm flesh of a baby
Who sleeps in the zoo

4 Like Mushrooms
Let's talk about love pats
Even if I kill you it's a love pat
Even if you fall down and hurt yourself
And bleed it's a love pat

5 Us Tasting the Air
For all I know
In twenty years
The tiger and the cougar
And you and I
We will all be
In Colorado
The best friends of the world

The Bicycle Rider

I see the winter turned around
like pleasure make the cabinet wail
when I open it, make the girls go
through the curtains again
and fold the shiny parts

The shiny roots are fired, the balls
in the sycamores
are swinging.
A talented bicycle rider
flew out of the winter for a sad party.

I'll stick that man in a tree,
especially without hooks,
without the jocks to meet those horrifying spooks,
like the bicycle rider
irrationally dropping his books.

POEMS FROM DEAL

(1969)

New World of the Will

A black ear crawls on the window. It is
my own, my very own remarkable ear.
I hear little of the original spirit.

A piece of paper caught up in a tree
bearing the stationary marks of you and me.
If you were here in teeth and kisses, in New York,

how would you see these animals, the ants,
how they teem and murder, and they are driven too?
It is time for the pronunciation of the will.

So here among the dull and nightly rocks,
here where we first met, with philosophy,
upon a lake where oarsmen rowed them past—

Receiving the strict letters and in the morning
on this same spot again I hinder you.

In Memory of Your Body

Your body has narrow slits instead of windows. And inside, your brain
turns around, silent. The more mouth you have the more pleasure.
Your eyes look like stables, look like dungeons, though they are
hard and white, of course, as your legs. Nor are those legs without
ornament: Two chains of great size and rotundity keep you prisoner.
Loitering on the beach, one common night, they were recognized and
stopped. In another corner of your body, a fountain spouts. Then there
are your breasts, which, carved in stone, would be thought wonderful
for miles. Everything around appearing a little abstract! I loved you,
so I carved your hands small and perfectly clean. They must not be
forgotten. And here I beg permission to close a chapter of still life.

The Heavenly Humor

Light became audible, that is, a child, and took the empty place.
Farther back, majesty was a leek to eat. Why make a younger mom
The thunderbolt of something quick go the round of her lover?
To themselves, they would guard it,
Fall upon a ray like the earless. Conquests or a new baby?
What has happened to Tommy, his violin and bow, must be wedded soon.
You must strike a beam.
Since childhood I sat down, sleeve across mouth.
What cannot be streaked over corpse grey in the land of rectangles.
Drenched?
Before the fire? Among airmen, entrusted to slaves,
I hope the peril in the ice will "experience" him.
And he was angry, lifted his eyes to the dangers of the mountains.
My desire sings admirably well but the mail-pilot
His belt—the toll-gatherer—sometimes does.
What, they ask, is this science?
Up the dead lane are forty-seven wings. We withdrew, killed his lift,
Sold olives, beans, unleavened paste.
They're all mad, leading me into the inappropriate feeling range.
A gleam hangs on the lips of a warmer sea
Simple as Plato taught, to be forbidden dream
Noon-tide light, broad daylight, manipulating the pulleys,
Crying, "His mistrust leaves it to the world"
All about vibrating surfaces—Oh yes
To buy a sound mantle for every strong man
The gallery filled up with stony variations of the Main Cashier
He endured until the next day when the longest lull occurred
My diagnosis suffered from an air of posing
He charged my toll "Why, good evening"
Very famous, he loves it, anything frantic with grief
It's noon-tide in Corsica
This is a woman's point, and David's point, expecting to find her husband
Shut your eyes, furbish
Musical drums, post-horns, sordines, all she was doing was music.
More remote, living safely together,
Girls often suggest men glance at the chalcography shop
Past times show bands—should in time be sunlight,
Incurious, exclusive,
Today, a fade into the glare
With reference to a particular period,
And with sparkling desire expected to come crashing through the floor.

Poems from Deal

1.

How wonderful to be in the arms of cerebral creatures.
You taste garage, moon, strength.
You have only a live child and fresh water on your arms.

2.

You take back. The hot shower drum roll.
    In that echo chamber, musicians have
showered. Evenings they swing up the vulture's
beak. But you fight with your teeth,
resuscitating few beaks. Why not fight me
in the Venus flower way. I'm happy for the anger
    you showed your room. Hating shining hating.

It's your Easter face. Face of Rose Island.
    The one face left in the book. "A vicious whisper
left her." Your sickness excites me of course
but why passive, why churning, does the world—
    do you insist on taking away the string?
It CEASES to vibrate. Now you accept David.

3.

The horse stamps
    across the beach:
a passive part.

Did you ever read the wet page of the earth?
not in this bodiless activity scored for instruments
half of the earth brings behind curtains because of
the heat: violin, tuba, bassoon. A dim page.
She said nothing slipping inside the streak except
"One day you will forget the land of rectangles."

4.

the book: "July 27. Trapped a blue
             butterfly after a red monarch."
the boy: "Open your wings, you stupid
             bitch."

the butterfly: "The boy whose comics these are
                    please advise him that I did."

    5.

Julie I want to gather your finely spun
your white lips. You had my son in February
back to my confused and situational room. That night
it rained in Switzerland; the entire land bounced.
I spoke to Uncle Louie of the Deal Bridge.
He said I could pass like the dead, very merry.
I want to rest your head.
Now only delicious cinders can rest there.

    6.

It is a powerful control.
Whenever. Not explaining. But hating shining hating.

The law of return prohibits
building the Apartments I never salvaged.

You can't believe that the process is cheap: the
process of shining. You don't love me
my pants and shoes that are curtains
cleats of desire; crease
that destroyed the bulwarks at Deal.

      "For every sandpiper there's a Giant Dirigible Sound"
      "Never better" "Never together"
      "They dragged physique out of the Atlantic"

"Then kissing her cheerfully, I gave her 'Peace with Love'"

    7.

I find a hopeless Haus in the picture, every time.
That forest! That Old Aged Home of Arizona!
They were rocking their boy again, out of the oven
into the monsoon.
"Taft believes in cherry fascism."
"Violet night-lights degrade trains."

8.
I discovered the United Nations night building.
It was a low-slung bar.
News on an electric band ordered one to
DEFINE THE PLACE: DEFINE THE TIME.

Napoleon used to persuade me to shinny up
long poles that always drop back from heaven.
What is the pacifist nutrition?
RHYTHM AS MENTALITY: RHYTHM AS SENSORY CONTROL

Why do we invent communities
in the clouds? their strictures against children
posted in the castles at Deal:
WALK ON THE MATTRESSES; DON'T WAKE THE BABIES.

9.
At the eighth storey window, what did I see?
What does fresh earth smell like, after a lightning storm?
"Above me the green leaves; below me my blue jacket; I forgot;
And now I'm freezing."
What is the test for people who heal?
for people who roll in the street?

  This then sir was my trial demand:

10.
When I was fifteen, my hands bounced. What was I reserving
for myself?

A hatchet to cut the waterfall away. Wonderful.

I walked past a ruling family. Distinguished
myself from conspiring friends. Can a kid look at a
kiss? You taught me the prose monodies. You taught
me the spelling stories. You didn't appear to be there.

To My Dead Son

I.

We muffle whatever is ripe. Then light up their lives in pastry
the cold nasal cone, the fluffy faces. Yes, you have beaten your way
to a cup, showing how to lug a vendetta halfway up the mountain.
Who was coming? A monster doing presto, through the green moss
thence to her private verandah on the stiffening porch. "She dallies
in a private parade, her human in a circle of moss." Her human star
quintuplets launched in a private parade. Her showed her the circle.
The shape of a shell. The vulva of a pig. Gate of composition
(as in a mine) returning after the work shift. Pillory 1.
Bullets are not scattering over the plants. March is carving. This
forms a thin hard crust. Young idiots cannot recover in the next ring
what would be most agreeable, given for free and nothing, delicious.
So I said, "My cap of green, my cap is cut. Record this terminable
light, the tutti I played on the banjo of light and zinc . . ." Ebb.
Evidently there are days that assemble in the desert, demand summits
say Virgil—but what I saw was a limp crocodile walking in eternity.
A choppy sea, partly blind, wholly blind. Then the ultimate principle:
a feeble light arouses the universe of gray-white. Statements:
"Feeling so great, the penumbra has featured its own veto"
"She is the articulate companion, she embraces her bowels"
"The heartwood lumber of the yellow birch divides in the springtime"
"You cheat your legs, you make new complaints from the uterus"
"The pale blue falcon suppressed a smile after being stuffed"
"It comes from Malheur and it makes a new edition of the Malebranche"
So leave your baby in the pond which I will sketch on your skin
under which the bones. Do you fall persistently, will you rush?
All roads to Deal have dried up, return to your wings. The state of one
Dead is not locating, exploding is not the underwater near the sea.

II.

   1.

I kept spinning in all kinds of grass. An unmarried woman
came and pointed out the stems to me. In my light fast
motorcycle, she read each letter in order. My hands are
resting on an arched roof, horse allowed to roam at night.

2.

She gave me a damp cheek, to explain why her copy didn't
fly through the night. The telephone operator heard a
coin. "This is very good." A bread accused me of the
hatefully long absence. In this, was I fit to be imitated?

3.

A soft unbleached ape in the carburetor due to weak
mixtures, while being launched. You blunt-nosed dolphins—
Decorating hat, shoe, etc. Who supported the vessel
while being launched? The Bishop of Rome of gas and air.

4.

The peony is a plant with showy flowers, no it is a race, a community
stocked with irritable qualities of red, pink, and white.
So back to the rules of penance, that shed standing with its roof
against the higher wall. "Enter a place . . . somewhat purple."

5.

She gives body to the words. She will come into the camp of
retired governors, she will insert herself between the mold and
the emotion. A girl ran away from the ice.
A husband carries on, I love you, the tide of the river said.

6.

The course of life on earth tends to repay an injury in kind.
"She made him quiet,
she will again, stars finding amends in stagnation."
Gravel is the ship's bottom. and the fireplace its frame of bars.

For the Princess Hello

Bridges that, a little because of absence,
Have like circuses changed their sites,
And the wood rots due to circumstance,
And, I believe, because of their engagement
To light, and something like light,
Whose voltage will run dry,
These bridges come like all bridges
To change and be re-painted.

Stone cries when it spans a void,
Wood thinks about the last century,
Both hate each other by custom
And can't contain their mountainous
Duality, like a turkey with two feathers
Pushed by the wind, turning
Into feathers of nothing without sweat:
A turkey's definition of change.

The old bridges faint under caresses,
Discovering the constant in a circle
Around forty-seven plane figures
Which they invented in foreign ports;
The liar and his lie
Win over a racially mixed city!
And these bridges come like all bridges
To change and be re-painted.

It's sweet to follow the trace of a bridge
And get angry without knowing why
Which one of the architects will succeed
In vaulting, character, and facing.
All the days of nine committees
Have been concerned with city bridges!
Now you will see the proof
That each has been re-painted.

Both stone and wooden bridges promise
Elevated above us, to separate
The hardened student from the breaths
Of a young girl, mouth open:
Each conserves the advantage
Of forces despite everything you say
In each of your false languages:
In its turn will be re-painted.

Master Canterel at Locus Solus

1.

And nothing was missing
Introduced into the brain
The family is now watching
The scene that's produced

The scene that's produced
Might be several different scenes
Once the muscles are loosed
With vitalium and resurrectine

With vitalium and resurrectine
They dress as they need to
Outside the cooling machine
Inside the grieving family

Inside the grieving family
Covered with heavy sweaters
And the wig they wear is heavy
Then they leave the ice-box

Then they leave the ice-box
And the laboratory technician
Takes a key and locks
After the end of the cycle

After the end of the cycle
There is no putrefaction
But that invariable cycle
Of the animated corpse

Of the animated corpse
He must document everything
He identifies the corpse
And he surrounds the corpse

And he surrounds the corpse
Puts walls where it falls
Puts stairs and chairs
Using originals if possible

Using originals if possible
He repeats indefinitely
The same scene in his skull
Chosen once forever

Chosen once forever
His eyes, working lungs, words
Actions, walk, as ever
And nothing is missing

2.

For perfection in prognostics
I imagined an apparatus
That the sun and wind would fix
The sun and wind combined

The currents of the atmosphere
But how they could give birth
To an art work was not clear
Only a fine mosaic would do

I searched for a material
That would engage the sun
And disengage my own will
And used multicolored teeth

That I had learned to attract
As you attract the breath
Attract rather than extract
Like wind to a balloon

Almost bloody roots
Immense molars and monstrous canines
And a milk tooth that shoots
An imperceptible light

A brusque and powerful magnet
That the world obeys
And the sick tooth drawn to it
Leaves the mouth without torture

Thus the toothaches stop
And the inferior maxillary
And tooth filling drop
Down the unwooded esplanade

At times bleeding, then brilliant
From the roots and cavities
I have furnished a monument
Where I found myself

Beyond this region of teeth
There is a single red root
The dove made of white teeth
Graciously flies to it

Mornings the mirror turns east
Dawn it contemplates the south
Nights the mirror shines west
And directly receives the sun

Elegy to Sports

Orestes pointed out what was despotic
    In youth and stingy hunger.
From his golden injuries he got
    What he wanted from you.

The key used to dial was at last in place,
    The house asbestos.
And he dressed up like a piece of human candy
    With great hustling.

Last stop! Your clothes fill up the trunk
    With a pitiful hand.
The seer in old age follows the raindrops,
    Touring an inhuman scene.

The Swiss have no wars, though they lose combats,
    The English are hemmed in by waves,
Those who drink the rivers Po, Tagus, and Danube
    Are found on the river bottom.

And so the vaulter, who rebounds into gravel
    Dragging his pole behind,
Like gasoline sets the hurdles on fire
    Jumping and jumping again.

The pianist whistles during the accompaniment;
    Mrs. closes her eyes;
She retires from us, seeing you dislike her
    And her rowboat collection.

Now you are happy, and you are more than happy,
    You swan of Lancaster.
Don't complain about the dull apartment life
    A thousand times a day.

The gnome brought suit against the cedarwood,
    And Libya owes money to a tree.

Your father has received the gems amber and garnet
    For a year's work on his bed.

You beat your hand, you jump out of line,
    And you say among yourselves:
"This is what Italy and Greece dumped on us
    In a thousand poems."

So you give away your violin, the other his trumpet;
    The girl gives you away.
And the women, the pedestrians, and the detective
    Desert the champ.

Ode

Permit me to take this sleeping man
And I will help him on his way.

Even with Be and Ice, my head
Bowed down as if I were sleepy.

If I could describe how Frank's
Eyes fell asleep, on hearing of Frank,

Like a painter working from a model
I could show how I went to sleep!

In my ramblings I closed my eyes
And transmuted thought into a product.

Moving in a trance with a keen face
I fell, and what happened to me

She knows who did this: She took my head
And held it down until I swallowed.

A girl walked by and said: I am Julia,
Open your eyes and see who I am.

When I heard this invitation,
She and my sleep went away together.

I have something of New York in me,
Lying against cement to bring it back.

There was almost no time between one "when"
And the other, I mean the "when" of waiting

And the "when" of seeing a woman in bed.
Thus, in presenting sleep

The poem must leap over the cut-offs.
You see clearly in a revolution,

Look down and notice how you have slept.

A MAN HOLDING AN
ACOUSTIC PANEL
(1971)

A Man Holding an Acoustic Panel

1. The Danube Loophole

On the ship there is an international airport.
Here, their passports are taken away from them.

These walls, these acoustical bricks, protect the man holding an
acoustic panel against a wave of shock and sound.

Ordinary microphones don't hear it, only the microphones with
"great surface" permit us to—Walls and closets will not stop
it—we will take these sounds to our grave.

Hearts working with determined frequency like twenty hearts, hands
black as glands.

The heart contracts to the accompaniment of electric phenomena. Here
is a microelectrode penetrating into the heart of a dog.

2. Flowers of the Mediterranean

Out of the car so old it is growing mushrooms, you emerge with a
vivarium to say: Here are anemones laid at leisure and daisies
in an inch of earth.

Figs and olives making insignificant profits. And these are vegetables
in a basin called a port. Fish in frenzy, open to the sky.

I overlooked the apples, the authentic apples being the "little
apples." Here are giant fennel renewing in a radical way. And
here's the squirrel, expecting to be fed.

The squirrel jumps on the customer, actually tasting him, locked
onto his chest. The Food and Health people are taking inventories
of this squirrel atrocity.

We could only sketch it. An island does not work. Delos didn't
produce (much).

3. The Hundred Years' War

Precisely because the wave has no echoes, the wake is second-hand.
Your ego was built that way. But the accessory non-ego
Is original to you like your near-silk ape-ware for the strict at heart
Àpropos of the motion picture On All Fours.

What the fisherman threw at his wife is hung up like a fiddle;
There is Father shaving in the sawdust; and Grandma holding a simple
    candle;
Mules, zebras, and Jews in the omnium gatherum in the midst of Russia.
And the century I live in turns out to be the century of infibulation and
    fuck.

Now we are lying securely, though broken into shivereens.
Your eye has been bandaged, the door locked, we're tied up like Rome
    and Greece.
But what will we use for the gashes; stickum, library paste, or fish glue?
Uncle John Chagy is playing the piano.

An angel visits, it has gleaned from one pile many snowballs.
And other snow collectors bunch up by the sexy stream.
I am ready to burst, like a whole class in revolution.
And in the center you come into focus, harmless as per usual.

4. Statue of a Breeze on Horseback

In a corner of air
On a couch built of air
We make a very little angle
Between "diode and triode lie near together

Are you in the corner of meteors?
You're in the crust of the earth
You have not yet extinguished the light complex in me
On my languorous couch of air

Air, which is alternately
Black and brilliant and crushed like a coin
That lies under the rocks at Deal
Normal as a neighbor and more clear

You are here
Here is the debut of culture
Here is your light face which Michelson and Morley followed
Here are the spores." Sir Alexander Fleming.

5. The Blocks of Accommodation

Everything was commonly regarded as fresh air: as if they had
privately appreciated the Fun Palace

And were now heading back for the Wet Factory alongside.

Nevertheless it was surprising a man twenty years old could
be a twin in another house,

Recognising that concrete starts as a slumpy aggregate and ends,
after the impression of being held shuttering together

At the height of one shuttering, as a garden soup, contributing
very little to the suspended street and fallibility.

The question being an almost unpierced, "Why don't you fall
through the floor?"

Postwar architecture will have no more colors, etc. Shh,
wait until I put it together again

So deviously devoted to the powers of the earth, the accommodation
required:

Rodney Grab, Shirley Bailey Flint, Chris Van Love,

Hotel Dionysus, Hotel Neon, Hôtel San-Rival, Hotel Jason,
  Hôtel Le Délicieux.

6. Cosmografia e Geografia

Yes, you can teach descriptive geography forever;
Corn correlations, too, but the correlations are always suspect.
You who can dance better than the other dancers
Will find out, though a lot later, you have received this as a prize:

Mountains, for example, like cement thermometers;
Men taking their human body temperatures
Beyond the range of ordinary thermometers
And the arid little mouse who drinks not at all,

And others who have learned to avoid baboon bands.
In Death Valley you stretched out in the shadow of your vehicle.
The Placebo Effect took its effect.
But you didn't wish to take advantage of these centers of advantage,

These water-catchers. Satisfied specifically
With the remote chance to discover the earliest anything . . .
And so we walked, Mr. and Mrs. Royal Eagle, with the roses and
    sensations
On the ground and with losses scattered erratically in the sky.

7. Conception Days

For the woman concerned
    for those fertile days

Dr. Kyasaku Ogino
    and Dr. Hermann Knauss

Have turned the outer barrel
    for your crystalline bodies

Much better than a pocket sundial
    or a *multiplicateur enfantin*

Blaise Pascal,
    add it up!

In the majority of colors too
    Red green and blue

Skipping through the window I encountered you
    Only slightly "polarised" as a result

8. The Mind of a Mnemonist

When I was two or three years old
I was taught a Hebrew prayer
But all I saw was the steamy word
That puffed and splashed the air

Presented with the lowest tone
I saw a sizeable ship
Though it gradually took on
The color of a *beep beep*

Presented with a higher pitch
I had a sense of taste
Like sweet and sour borscht
Gripping me around the waist

With a tone pitched higher
I saw a woman in red
Fading without humor
As she got into bed

Presented with an amplifier
I saw her velvet "cord"
And the Strangler fraying its fibre
With his unpleasant pink finger

Presented with stronger amplitude
It looked like a skin disease
Or like frankly rough food
I hurt my teeth on this

Presented with more decibels
I saw lightning split heaven
As if someone thrust orange needles
Into my streaky spine

At three thousand cycles a second
I saw a fiery broom
And the whisks were sweeping around
A fiery room

I took a mental walk
With you New Year's down Broadway
We had a long white talk
And your voice was a bouquet

In my father's bookstall
My father could locate any book
But my mother erased them all
So her son could become classic

9. Master of the Seedboxes

Fear and relaxation, anger and anxiety,
Panic and coordinated motor activity,
Cannot take place at the same time!
He lived on his free ticket twenty years,
The Honorable, the Master of the Trains,
Saying, Transparency is a merit in itself,
Economy is a merit in itself. Inversion
Is that a merit in itself?
When he changed trains, as in Turin,
A cultured figure turned pomegranate, he died.
How does it feel like to be dead, Ron Padgett?
I know you'll know the right word or bullshit it.
And what is the brightest thing in nature?
If we all looked at our penises, we'd all see things.
        In the train at Skopje you learned an important word:
Breakfast. A thunderous hour: as lightning struck
You released the boy's hand, thus saving your life,
The wonder of flying above the scene, you know serene.
Mulling over last night's TV at the American Cemetery
With apples that they throw away in Israel.
Like a repair man who relaxes and remembers a freezer
Which he has prepared for the whole family
And the kitchen gets ready and fruit begins to freeze,
Aphrodite soon played an extremely important part.
        The Master of the Seedboxes was heartbroken.
In the *Shorter Guide to the World's Flora*
I had left out Madagascar. Oh why do most people think
Most botanists are dull? Langsam, Roger.
The ostraca were apparently prepared in advance
Of the voting day, but were not used.
This cemetery is like a farm, hay grows
Between the graves, and you have to harvest it.

10. In Human Hair

In 1831, when glass curiosities known as "Friggers" were made by crafts-
men for amusement and tests of skill, little Emily Shore was taken.

She wrote, "He made glass baskets, incandescent birds and candid horses.

He set a table like a treetop and before him burned sticks of every size and color.

I saw lace bobbins inscribed Dear Harriet, Aunt Jane, Jack's Alive, and George; and wooden bobbins with pewter inscribed Constant Prove To Me My Love and plain bobbins inscribed George.

She saw his picture embroidered in human hair, commemorating his sparrow pots built into the garden walls to encourage the birds.

They nest there rather than the roof, providing him with an easy means of obtaining an oblong full of young birds for sparrow pies per dozen dead sparrows.

He kept his man trap called "the humane" in the kitchen, with the candlesticks, early matches, and triple dead fall mouse traps, with the mouse already crushed.

This trap replaced the earlier one with interlocking "candid" teeth which has been declared illegal.

"At night I played tennis and saw the racquet for real. There is one real tennis court in Cambridge, off Grange Road. Afterwards we went to the biscuit shop at Castle End and saw a hornet die, weighed on the Baker's Doughnut Scale.

The lamp in which the lard so often burned enabled Miss Caldecote to inspect the inside of her mother's large oven and see whether her bricks were in good repair.

And I have seen the Poison Bottles–Not To Be Taken. These were sexy six-sided bottles containing irresistible poison no longer made, since harm has been replaced by plain white ones which are however still. Ridges on one side guide the people with poorer sight.

Past the first fire insurance office, called "The Fire," formed in 1630 after a fire, with iron fire marks on the wall, inscribed FIRE and LIFE.

In the evening, Emily had a dream about the peace of the eighteenth century:

First one on the beach was Walter dear with a King George jug (mss. on the back asking for you).

Second was Queen Anne with commemorative china and one of her feminine messages (mensonges) saying, "Once we were the tools and we will be the utensils, too."

They were all eating gingerbreads baked and covered with gold leaf, hence the expression "naked and deaf as the gingerbread," but their hair sieves were replaced by modern time sieves.

The powder from their wigs was being blown way out over the waves by the Powder Blower and the excess powder disposed by shaking the wigs into the wind.

"I saw all the wits of the century attached to a mechanical "Jack" in which their collective "je" was descending like so much weight after being wound up.

And Dante was spitting in front of a fire with a revolver in his hand, allowing them, the damned, and a little meat placed in front of them, to be "cooked to a turn."

I woke up and picked up my silver Mesh Bag to strengthen myself with a handkerchief. The silver will not discolor; I have lined the bag with your hair.

11. The Racquet for Real

"Here, candlesticks are bedrooms.

We are being carried upstairs again, with the candles already lit, the mouse already crushed with a triple dead fall in the mouse trap.

The early matches are indeed extinguished and we two little people keep working on the dust in the kitchen, operating the bellows and boosting the pedals.

Dust collected in that bag will be contained in the box of this Zorst Vacuum Cleaner, inscribed *Constant Prove To Me My Love*, best worked by two people."

12. The Earthly Way

> About yesterday
>> It was in the 90's and I didn't know what to play
>> I'm not Antigone throwing the dirt
>> I'm my hot and bored little sister throwing grass
> No I'm the kids from the end of the block
>> And I make a big leap in hopscotch from 1 and 2
>> To 6 and 7 (Why don't I ever take
>> The Earthly Way?) and I slip
>> And I've skinned my ankles
>> But I'm all right now
>> Love your sister

13. The Apparition of Pullulation

A child comes home and tells his mother the teacher will give him some marks. But it is not true; the teacher will give him no marks at all, either good or bad.

And we know nothing except that on the face of it 150,000 years ago an Englishman said *Doodledoo* and a French girl said *Cocorico*.

But as with Frederick the Great and Machiavelli there was not the same financial power at their disposal. The Americans became American all over.

The cricket was fertile mostly during the years of paradox when it was rare and alone.

The bee could not distinguish but it could prefer. Her body soaked in the flower, was impregnated with it. Then she regurgitated it to the other bees, the bees of India who only dance on a horizontal plane.

You agree, so the museum director helps you with the *Apparition of Pullulation*, a device enabling you to "hear" a fable of La Fontaine said in most languages. This is *Le Corbeau et le Renard* in Yugoslavian, the language of your choice. And you thought it was broken!

The electric fish have made the plunge; all is quiet now except the breathing torpedoes.

Now it is a quarter past three. No it is not quarter past three, it is quarter to three. It's hard for a leper to have a hypochondriac for a friend. Now it's half past five.

14. The Lottery of Heredity

Mother is represented by her twenty-three pairs of chromosomes.
Baby is represented by a Ciceronian legalist with an electric drill.
Dad is represented by twenty-three pairs of painted chromosomes.

Normal teeth, a memory for some colors, RH factor, a tendency
    to varicose veins, fingers maybe. Insensibility of the bladder?
    No, of taste. Normal fingers, black hair, normal urine, normal
    nose, family life.

Mother is exposed at 11:15, 3, and 5:15.
    Baby is never touched.
Dad appears to be praying:

"If he happens to have those two traits, he won't make it
past one year of life."

15. The Maryland Sample

This butterfly cluster suggests a way to get at American "makers" more directly. The coldness of these showers is very encouraging. Other bug reducing techniques (latent animate wingedness or bee-cluster analysis of a kind like that used by Pleasant and Rough 1960) may be even more appropriate. How quiet your smile is, when it happens to carry along with it the noon, the day, the hmm, the smile of the day, the deaf man holds an ordinary telephone in his hands and hears the dashing of oars in the Thames not the "Handicap March." How swift and bitter these questions are, because they are partially immersed in the Atlantic and micro-organisms must feed on: he, it, them, they:

> "Because the bitter bee deceived us
> Because we obeyed the quiet bug
> Because we restored the rough butterfly
> Between the smooth cocoon and the pest
> The needle was swift we hadn't time to inquire
> How swift the needle is as we examine it
> How thirsty the net is as we gallop into it"

16. Untitled

The marks, tears and wipes of wonderful early works have turned
　　　　to a more harmonized Mutism.
Finding in the scrupulous self-portraits, now double,
　　　　disappointed awe harassed by jerks.
Now from the fingers on old tickets; now from young men dying to
　　　　conduct; now from a season's free ticket; now from the fungus and
　　　　neglect.

Blocked, vexed, and aggrieved,
　　　　at the height of passion
　　　　when the vaulter might leap
they cut the channels
of the soft wind-pipe.

It's sweet to the sweet
　　　　always carrying a brunt
　　　　for that sacred top
In man it's self-willed
　　　　perpetually giving a shake

17. The Funeral of Jan Palach

When I entered the first meditation,
　　I escaped the gravity of the object,
I experienced the emptiness,
　　And I have been dead a long time.

When I had a voice you could call a voice,
　　My mother wept to me:
My son, my beloved son,
　　I never thought this possible,

I'll follow you on foot.
　　Halfway in mud and slush the microphones picked up.
It was raining on the houses;
　　It was snowing on the police-cars.

The astronauts were weeping,
　　Going neither up nor out.
　　And my own mother was brave enough she looked
　　And it was all right I was dead.

18. Ode

James Bond's girl friend
Lay in bed, having
A bad dream during a thunderstorm
All the leaves came falling down:
Two men in space,

A lady and her dog,
A lady and her baby,
A tree house, little huts and boats,
And men caught birds
To take to another country

Aaron stayed in the temple
But Mrs. Grub went to the dentist
Leaving her boy with chickenpox
It was raining on the houses
It was snowing on the police-cars

And so the birthday girl
Who drags her hair
Down down down to the practice mat
Unwinding the serpent power
Of her spine behind her

Hears the owl
That hoots no more
Dazzled by headlights as it were
And swept across the road, the tree empty,
And the mind emptier than ever before, and freer.

Taking a Look

Nobody doubts
that it is snowing now

Rounding out their interpretation of the month

February, here is our
formal sketch

Everybody concedes a certainty to this snow

The upshot of which is NOT thrown projection

Well, or definitely not "disclosedness"

Again and again, February

This winter irretrievably put aside

Taking a look
It shows we have clung to idle talk *all right*

"I'm going to write a little thing
About Nothingness"
"Go ahead dearie"

And curiosity *would* be giving out summer information

The cars confine themselves
to the lot
Which is also the foundation for our feet
Now being covered up
In the sense of flakes
The driver weakened
And the certainty of being covered up

About a Farmer Who Was
Just a Little Boy

with Renée

Once there was a farmer
  and a farmer fell in a pot of water
    and a farmer was dead
  and then he came back alive
   and then he was never, never dead again
  until once in a thousand of years

After that he was sad
  because he didn't get his own way
  because he was only a farmer

He met a wife
The wife was a bride
and the bride had a wedding
After that
the bride come home with his father
  and the wife was finished with his work
and he ate as much dinner as he could

    He blew up to be BIG BIG BIG
He was as big as my daddy
  After that he met lots and lots of people
at the wedding anniversary
And they all sang "About the Bride"

    And the farmer was there
      Everyone was there except the farmer
      Because the farmer was only a little boy
    And the bride blew up
    To be as big as my daddy
    So the farmer couldn't come
      Because the bride was a big lady
    Because the bride was the farmer's mommy

Then after that after a couple of years
    He was sad because he wasn't a bride anymore
    The farmer didn't have a daddy just a mommy
Because the daddy died, his name was Jonathan
    Then the bride Stevie was a farmer
And so the bride took off her clothes and went outside
    to play and took a walk to the store, the A and P

After that she was happy
    because she had a little boy who did the right things
and he never got spanked again
        Then the next morning he went outside by himself to play
        Then she went in the street and Tommy got hit by a car
So the farmer got hit by the car
    So his mommy got worried about him
        Because he didn't have a mommy anymore
    So after he didn't have a mommy
        Then, after that, Tommy was sad because he wanted his mommy
    And he didn't have his mommy
And he cried and cried and his mother didn't see him because he died.

The Destruction of the
Bulwarks at Deal

1.

Lord I sleep and I sleep

I am haunted all night by the look of cars

When I sleep they can speak, they say: Ride me,
    David. I am fast as death

Well who lighted this road up? Who made me this clear?

You know I am soft as plasma

I am haunted by all these things

I am crushed instantly

2.

Each considers himself at rest in the ether.

The red birds are dancing. They saw the sun! They
saw the sun! They call me, they call me the genius
of the lake.

The wild ducks are moving.

You are the only thing that is going to die today,
sick man.

You were the one that stretched the lake water.

You are the genius of the lake.

You were washed in the water drop. I need it, I
need it now.

Sick man, now you really have to leave me alone.

You made me make this up. You made me love music.

You told me: This is the music that weaves the Nest.

1960–1962

The Carburetor at Venice

I have had an accident. I cannot see.
I have broken my glasses and I've missed my train.
I like you very much. Do you like me?

I need a guide. I need a secretary.
For when? For tomorrow. I will come again.
I have had an accident. I cannot see.

I need an interpreter. Here is my key.
Ouch! Stop! How long will it take? Please use novocaine.
I like you very much. Do you like me?

Remove your clothes. Open your mouth and lie
Like an interesting city under an airplane.
I have had an accident. I cannot see.

The battery is dead. Charge up the battery.
Can you draw me a little map of the road I'm on?
I like you very much. Do you like me?

Can I see you today for the whole day? How long will that be?
Here is a present for you. A silver brain.
I have had an accident. I cannot see.
I like you very much. Do you like me?

THE PAGE-TURNER
(1 9 7 3)

The Page-Turner

"Perhaps we can imagine a book like this one. . . ."
—CLIVE KILMISTER, *The Nature of the Universe*

The cover of the book is itself exactly
Page one is you within a small room
Page three already a fair field for your tomb
Page four contains Newark matter-of-factly

Page five appropriates all its frightening streets
On page six Greater Manhattan glumly fits
There is room on page seven for all deceits
And on page eight the earth comfortably sits

And now the pages get much more inspiring
We turn again and not much can be seen
Though on page ten the moon begins soaring
Into details, darkness comes in on page eleven

On page twelve we see bodies not unlike
Our body, let's leave them at this stage
Now we can see the sun the first star for our sake
That moved us from the center of our page

Like us the asteroids are always travelling
And other rocky lumps that never waver
And now miles are an inconvenient thing
The traveller ages less than the observer

That solar system has withered to a dot
And we've been turning pages for light years
By twenty-two your naked eye is shot
By all the naked stars when night was yours

Naked-eyed page-turners around the world,
Turn very rapidly to page twenty-three
Two dinner plates is our galaxy
Vague whiteness in which the main course is still veiled

Let's turn one more page, page twenty-five
Now we are the cluster known as Local Group
Moving hither and thither as if alive
And we are, some stars, others merely hot soup

On page twenty-seven we approach the limit
And we are neither unique nor rare
No matter how far we go into it
At the end of our amazement is distant air

Now we really seem to be near the end
Covering one more page at enormous speeds
And what can we expect, from our imaginary hand
On page twenty-eight, when all we see recedes?

The Music Stand

On the music-stand the music stands like softened skin.
And outside the peony, burning with silent thirst.
You in rayon with your ton of discs frisk in the garden
Playing an artificial Eskimo basketball with leaves that rust.

There is no saucer of love for the peony,
Only a little brutal water from pipes.
The sink was on fire, death to all leaves, Mother sleepy,
As Autumn flagged or breezed out near the pumps.

Come and go, my numina, ransack the music!
You were found unwilling to be snapped
With Her, hovering over such depths as bees among their own
       claque
As Judy danced behind the grillework.

With "your name on their stingers" they couldn't catch you
Apparently advancing to your own room
Slowly whirling the black Lazy Susan (you loved your own
       games)
Before malaise lit your head with an emotionless beam.

Then the ball would smash in, as if to prove perspective!
And the bell, and time to quit gym for orchestra
Wondering what your seat would be in the orchestra of heaven.
Oh my pianist, let me sit beside you as a page-turner!

You said, "The violinist does not like his repertoire tonight.
The pianist looks at the rented stool with some pain.
The page-turner, from Russia, faces his task with delight
And hopes he will be called to serve thus again.

"The violinist knows that the rehearsals before
Were too short; the pianist looks at the little shore
Of white keys and feels a most divided will.
The page-turner is at his highest peak still.

"The violinist lifts his violin, as if in a high wind.
The pianist also has treachery in mind
Placing one finger on the white part.
The page-turner is silent, in the best tradition of his art.

"A dinosaur attacks, only to be attacked in the back by a Rex
          and crushed
It is tragic for a girl to love in an attic
Filled with such plaster-of-paris, a warehouse of castaways
If noble, decomposing in the weather, where the maids have
          washed."

On the music-stand the music stands like softened skin.
The shuffling has stopped. I walk the plank.
I used to be a blank. And now I am a blank.
Oh my pianist, let me sit beside you as a page-turner!

The Night Sky

To look up in your face
Is like looking into the devastated night sky
Lights of all kinds I trace
Animals, battles, the whole picture rotating by

Now the nervous system is suspended
Your total mass enjoys recuperation
In repose our theories are almost ended
You are inert as Eve in hibernation

The sailors go to sleep, and then their sails
And then a dead ocean falls upon my mind
I think of grapes put to sleep or apples
Kind apples and night's welcome officer wind

Let us return now to your hair
So long and inconvenient
Fixed to you and waving like that slowly rotating star
Swept past one's vision to make a point

Sharp flashes of those eyes show you once a week
So well within the behavior which is yours
Deliberately trying to find someone else in the universe awake
Life, a long way ahead of ours

Your body is no bigger than the earth
Dreaming outside the sudden switch of the sun
Sending off attached clouds as little worth
And twinkling your closed eyes: their work is done

But not your lips triumphantly open
Musically since the ear is ready
Weightless as a knife in air will sharpen
And the billiard ball grow giddy

I would thread with a hook and eye your dress
Fasten you to me with a rod or bolt
Pass through like a curtain rod your eyes
And they never shut

You are relative to the distant stars
Not smeared out to a lump, a leaf
A lot of annihilation is going on, you cut your hairs
But the hair grows back and not the knife

We are fixed at both ends forever
In the frequency of the fundamental cave
Holding us is a musician however
Like a string and like a wave

On Becoming a Person

The night I decided to paradoxically intend
I had the wished-for bad dreams.
Elizabeth Bishop, whose "2000
Illustrations" this shows I had been reading
was whistling in a nightgown and playing and
singing to her family,
"I am the death tree,
I grow spontaneously,
I grow in the round,
Plant death in the ground"
after which duet
was played on the $59 Sony cassette
she became lugubrious, dramatic,
or conversely lubricated, and mellow,
and sighingly said,
Now I am going to bed, like a good girl!

In a sense, we are all child prodigies.
"I offer my frayed body to
              your corruscating soul
I open my used out eyes to your looming mouth
And my song which is yours in the
              old air of time
Big treaties on paper which fall from rock to rock"

A Problem

There are two ways of living on the earth
Satisfied or dissatisfied. If satisfied,
Then leaving it for the stars will only make matters
          mathematically worse
If dissatisfied, then one will be dissatisfied with the stars.

One arrives in England, and the train station is a dirty toad.
Father takes a plane on credit card with medical telephone.
One calls up America at three-thirty, one's fiancée is morally
          alone.
But the patient is forever strapped to the seat in mild turbulence.

Thinking of America along psychoanalytic lines, and then
                    delicately engraving nipples
On each of two round skulls
You have learned nothing from music but Debussy's ions
And the cover of the book is a forest with two lovers with empty
          cerebella.

Beyond the couple is a second girl, her head smeared out.
This represents early love, which is now "total space."
These are the ways of living on the earth,
Satisfied or unsatisfied. Snow keeps falling into the brook of
          wild rice.

A Family Slide

Family on the slide, you should say!
See if this slide fits—
It rained yesterday; it rained today—
I told you we had duplicates

Oh no it's in backwards
It doesn't matter
Debbie's right that's the reverse
It doesn't matter

Is this my 16th birthday
All my fancy friends
Judy looks gorgeous but her friends
All look strange—slender and vital is a cliché

Who are these people now?
People you no longer know.
Who are these old women?
Are they young women?

Stupendous horrendous tremendous.
And the fourth word is—hazardous!
Hazardous! hazardous! hunh! Everybody had a hint!
Just remember Mother had the same hint!

Is it a popular word, Walter, in everyday use?
It may not be in use everyday
But it COULD be in use everyday.
Momentous, bomentous . . .

Oh that's when we wanted Naomi to compete
In the Greenwood Pool contest
But she wanted nothing to do with it.
Good! "Why?" Why! We don't believe in a Beauty Contest!

("I believe in Beauty Contests.")
Who is this person?
That's you, and what's more that's me sitting behind you.
Know thyself, know thyself, is a famous expression.

Gnothi sauton, but who said it in English?
Pass the next slide please and don't ask who.
Don't worry about the viewer, the batteries are rechargeable.
Through photosynthesis, we're rechargeable too.

Once in a while Irv took a nice picture.
Like the one of Judy in Binghamton looking like a violin
And here is David playing on the shore
Mr. Eisenberg says, "Let me out and let the dog in"

Lao Tse said doing nothing was the way
To get along and little Debbie knows the dynasty
The bending reed won't break they say
But mother says, "If you bend it enough in the same place it may."

Father Knows Best

It is the old show, but the young son can fly.
He sees pink and blue and red umbrellas in the air.
They teach him how to fly.
Of course the family does not see and has resentments.

One day at a snow party he tries to prove he can fly.
But he only leaps a bit and loses the jumping contest.
Then Father realizes son must enclose but a few electrons
                    of air in his fist
Then son flies high above the family garage and trees,
                    branch by branch.

There are no umbrellas, there are only frosty parachutes,
Little angels who instruct him how to fly.
He must not struggle too much with his hands,
Which having practised the violin now dog-paddle in air.

High above the invigorated gulf the air walks down its
                    own road.
And sister jumps up in a dual column of wind.
Inside, Mother serves breakfast; the bluejay gulps at
                    the feeding-station.
The family now knows he can fly, but still father knows best.

View

When I was asleep you beat me
Happy in the laxity of night.
As Sophocles and Niobe cried out
Inert day put out its precursor's small quantity of light.

When we were mascot scouts like little leaves
Grandma propped on the sand like President Lincoln
The blimps paused above us with their tiny brakes
Last threads that held us to the sky!

I thought of you as frangible as badly broken reefs
Where Darwin's spirit sleeps and cannot wake any longer,
To observe this moth on the ceiling screaming with remorse:
Then his blue wisdom would be effaced; the Voyage of the
          Beagle without eyes.

Tonight the floor is full of fancy flowers from old brains
And a grainy aplomb as at the end of the world.
All tightness is slowed down and dipped into
          compromised ideas.
Golden uncertainty has given you time to decide.

Cascade

"Notre vie coule de roche en roche"
—*Reverdy*

I left my dilatory feet in the golden sand.
Nothing in normal light but a summer broken off:
You can still see the entire foot from the broken piece.
Alone and vague it hesitates to mount the boards.

The tree, encircled by vague moss, is inflated as if by disdain.
Not a word glides by that does not lose itself among cinders.
You laughed, your eyes lowered like the fire itself.
Finally it was necessary to go lower than your forehead: a
      curtain.

Surely the source of so much blood must be an event, if not
      blessing.
The axe among flowers is getting longer and longer:
Now it is two axes, carving out a portico as the sky burgeons
      and flees.
Then you lower all the eyelids, and we breathe together a long
      time.

It is always the same, the same foot stuck in the forest,
As one stumbles, the same bottles balanced on trees,
Craning your neck to look without pity at this rigamarole,
Character traits of our life, which run from rock to rock.

80 / David Shapiro

About This Course

The leaf twists and turns, then floats down the drain.
Surely in all nature there's no motion more ordinary.
And even if we were to describe it, what would we gain?

Each leaf would seem to require its own quatrain.
Indeed, this is typical of most earth events' individuality.
The leaf twists and turns, then floats down the drain.

And so, facing this dilemma, like the scatterbrain
We are, at least for a little while, we leave the leaf laboratory
And even if we were to describe it, what would we gain?

We want to describe motion, but the motions are insane
Typical of most earth events occurring simultaneously.
The leaf twists and turns, then floats down the drain.

The leaf like you in rain looks almost human—
Powerless, almost comfortable, as predicted by theory,
And even if we were to describe it, what would we gain?

You too seem to rot quietly on the proverbial vine
But like rifle bullets you vibrate incessantly.
The leaf twists and turns, then floats down the drain.
And even if we were to describe it, what would we gain?

That morning that we rolled our undisturbed
        path
Made clear what was really important: straight out
        into space
The balloon jumped forward and a little air spurt
        out
In the opposite direction: Our tug-of-war took us,
        two observers
You to the barge, I to the drifting shore: we each
        gave our report of the incident:
An apple and a kite and a negligible feather kept
        falling,

A man kept running into his tent; the field (which,
        sagging slightly, had been pushing up on your body)
Suddenly gave way—you hardly felt me falling beside
        you
But this does not mean I had lost my weight which could
        only happen if the earth were removed
Or shook back and forth sideways in far, interstellar
        space.

Weren't you surprised? You watched the
        frictionless device
And smoothly it glided along as after your
        slightest nudge.
It showed no sign of failing our everyday
        elation.
Yet it was behaving quite as naturally as
        a table.
Then you took off and glided across
        the floor,
Just like a dry-ice disk, as it challenges
        our notion of the natural.
The bluejay kept a moving worm from
        moving forever.
Of course the violin did not fall to the ground
        as soon as I lost contact with the bowstring.
But the sensation was of lying on a soft bed of sound.
        Weren't you surprised? "One beat of a fly's wing,
One pulse of a laser, the time between heartbeats,
        a strobe-flash duration"—The question is fair enough, but
                there is no answer.

The flame goes up and the smoke keeps travelling
        down;
The sun is in the zenith and the watery sap flows so
        abundantly from a cut branch: in a short time
It fills a glass and forms a cool
        refreshing beverage;
The flame goes up and the smoke keeps travelling
        down;
Actually a photo of you is being pushed across the sky,
        as if to fix everything;

Nevertheless one must get started on one's work and
        overcome by storm the shadows: it blows against us
And so the cars and pucks, that skid along, since the
        table or road is attached to the earth,
Are skidding toward the heat death of their
        world;
The entire earth is but a baseball thrown horizontally,
        our hands crumple up or smash up or dent
Or stick together and heat up and have their insides
        changed;
And we, like the water at the bottom of the waterfall, awake in
        anechoic chambers

I filled a swimming pool with chairs, and all
        who swim must dive between:
My father's viola, my sister's cello, my
        sister's violin,
My uncle's piano, my mother's piano, my sister's
        cello,
My father's violin, my sister's cello,
        my grandfather's voice.
I am not a meteorologist. I am a poet. Why? Well, in the
        fall the cricket is a better reader of heat than most.
Listen to a cricket for fourteen seconds; add forty; and that's
        the heat, that's how hot it is where the cricket is.
Now if the cricket sang 34 times in fourteen—sang how hot
        it is—how hot would that be?
Not too hot. Now I want to start my song "My butterfly,
        my bee."
Bufo americanus, throat of male, loose and dark, it may be
        heard of rainy nights

The first time we see we are standing in a
        windowless elevator
The elevator is falling through its shaft, falling,
        falling.
We keep dropping coins from our pockets to the floor,
        but the coins float away.
Then we throw our pens against the wall, but those pens
        never reach the wall.
We conclude we are in outer space, because there is no gravity.

But we are only standing in an elevator, falling,
	falling.
The second time we see we are in the same elevator,
	in the middle of outer space,
Drawn by a long cable, attached to some supernatural
	force, consistently accelerating,
We keep dropping our coins and throw our pens forward again—
	this time everything lands with a splat
We conclude we are only in an elevator falling through its shaft,
	but our legs feel heavy—we are really in space: the earth
		a pencil-dot.

Well-known largely because of my inability to fly, I have
	gained a place in the literature if not your backyard.
I have no noticeable wings or tails and since I am flightless
	I live on the ground.
We are related, but even this relationship is not close
	enough.
In a hole I am well-hidden. When young I closely resembled
	the adult.
Now that I am old I can run. Others can fly away, but require
	considerable area to get a running start.
But for you flight is easy. And you are more slender than
	these. "The ground dove nests on ground or in the trees."
We ourselves are fastened to opposite ends, your head
	adjustable from the outside
Carries a mirror so that it is kept steady: in this case I
	am exhausted, detecting a grain
Of repulsion: the pressure of two lamp-blackened
	lovers: the faces more heated than bright
Then the faces recede, as though repelled by light
	bodies, but this explanation is inadequate.

They treat us like dirt, and we are dirt too
	turning black at maturity with the skin stretched,
Like a somewhat tight glove which is forced upon the hand
	on the diamond, quantities of children running home,
But powerless to exempt themselves from falling clay,
	and from falling bats,
Consenting to this on their knees, the rudimentary
	club,
Lowered down as part of the weather uh . . .
	probably

Few persons escape, though it may remain very localized, like
        fingernail polish,
Those half-human features magnified: eyes at the top, ears at
        the side, and the mouth is lower down,
And as stars fall unproductively into the lake, no bigger
        than a woman's hand among cloven feet,
A rather attractive hand when opening among clouds, with
        chances to recover you in one piece, on the way to bat.
The eyes are vestigial. The nose is an ornament. And we will
        neither grow old nor look old.

Here, their passports are taken away from them.
        On the ship, there is an international airport.
The sperm whales float along, waiting their turn
        to be taken to the factory,
Verdicts are executed to the accompaniment of
        music, the boat is slow because it travels through
                restrictions,
Injured people confess they were born without arteries, and are
        arrested in hospital on grounds of carelessly causing death,
Ultrasonic impulses keep them crimped to a group. In exchange
        for a spic and span lunch which they enjoy
All the way downstream, taking advantage of
        the loopholes,
They are given a numbered ticket which allows them to land, at
        a duty-free shop to visit the folks for three hours,
But even while they wait they are marked with
        Roman numerals
They have used the bodies of children as improvised bridges,
        which they later cross.

In school they teach you about osmosis but not why things
        stick together
And they stick together because nothing else is between
        them.
We adhere because we are so close, and only because of
        that.
The stars go thoroughly into the sky. The youthful murderer
        is identified by his mother.
The gun is recovered from the interior of the
        television set

The pinpricks are so close together one feels only the one
        solitary pinprick.
And as the whale's stomach is split open, its last
        meal is revealed.
"I couldn't draw my mind but this was on my mind
        It was a horse maybe—it was you and me—
It was dirt—plunk—it was a sparkling round sleep-
        inducing diamond, from which thoughts
Departed according to their sizes. It was a horse
        of many holes, you see."
The hens lay eggs under the artificial light, believing
        that day has come.

The months had almost put a soft pedal on the mouth,
        but presently showing the cymbals' inner sides, in triumph
After clashing them, it might sound more like kerbang!
        or powie! It's the dead sound I'm trying to apply . . .
You like the agreement of sounds all right, but its history
        has been pretty resolutely purred or yapped out,
With my toot between your teeth and midday smelling of
        English kisses, *silentium altum* put the gag on you
A drum-head and drum-skin and a drum-stick already seen
        to split attention like a conch.
You are the prime work of God and you smell like a scent-bag!
So listen to the songish program
In which I am the sparrow and you the itinerant gleemaiden
        or streetsinger carrying sheet music up the smeared street.
And the music rolls past you as trees are tied up together
        and the past repeated by arrangement with the Conductor
And it is crying, to you, like a hurrah of tigers, in full possession
        of their faculties, unexaggerated animals, because weeping
                without
Reservation, by my troth, puffing and hot, as a confused ship is
        intimidated by the land which turns out to be compassionate.

The earth being both a lodestone and a
        baseball
Light bounces off the mirror. Light
        persists
But has to be given up in the long run, like
        little balls, as far too limited

We have lived by the light of this empty
    space,
This information of canvasses painted by
    beams,
Not by masters, unappreciated light because not
    easily separated from hide and go seek.
You played a truncated version, covering your
    eyes
Thinking that you could never be seen, as I see you
    now.
And we are skidding like a bullet in a
    tree stump
Entering at top speed but coming to rest like two pennies,
    one on top of the other.

The finest pencil one can imagine is just
    a shadow
A ray of light is something they invented to shoot
    bullets through without causing it to flicker
You can pass your hand right through the bulb
    without feeling a thing
It's the little lamp that isn't there, like the kilogram
    that carefully protected cylinder at Sèvres
With a bug on it, though I hate to say it, light
    which even if it doesn't fall at $45°$ is nonetheless light
Each clear evening discovering dozens if not
    hundreds of new stars
But we concentrate ourselves further on smaller and
    smaller mirrors
And eventually the mirrors are as small as a single false note
    interrupting a tiny dead day
What is light? Watch your feet, my data lie
    underneath them.
What is light? It is something different from all
    that we have studied.

We have been sailing in a certain small fountain,
    like physicists in toy boats
Each craft bears a candle on its deck. We light the
    candles and the boats puff by
As if you were real, delightful. And we who have never
    been able to resist

The course of a new toy dream have spent much time
        watching the fun in the fountains.
And if we, in a sense, sink in that water,
        the goldfish, I am sure, will retain
Their silver dignity. We are fed beside the
        fountains
As the young are fed by the experiment and the
        results.
It confirms us; and now the whole water
        is silver;
A crucial step is taken, but years
        later,
The fountain is slowed down, as if controlled
        by your calm hands.

LATENESS
(1977)

Music Written to Order

Now and then, now and then, now and then
Now-ness and then-ness
And between now and then
You hear the sound of a projector
And revisit your ancient home, your new home of late.

You find only the gardener's sun has survived,
A detail that wanted to be a Psyche
Writing daily squibs to the dead.
A white breast on a white nipple would make a nice sculpture.
But you would want more milk.

You would want Mother back.
You go where you must go, Naomi goes
With Ruth, the record with the record player
Adults move magnetised to the earth.
All other insects forage at random . . .

Yes the early Christians wore masks
And had listened to Terence
Accounting for the look of no look
Cubicle said to be that of Love and Psyche

Consciousness you loved
Rounds you preferred
Sliding into the sky, looking wearily past the pink
                              toward the white
Where everything is unsigned, unsinged

In the life of the individual as well as the state
everything is late
An old vine on three stories
Of brick administration building that cannot administrate

Snow in the strictest sense
Snow so grasped I could hold to be a fiction
We profited by the wind
Twining up a rainspout, a wire, or the chain link fence

Through persian blinds again
Big emphasis on little jealousies
Taking the part for the part again
Is it rain or ripples on that stream of sphinx white paper

Inside, the unknown girl in a circle
Looks shyly down
Bone necklace and ghostly braids seeping
Into the blue air of the postcard

A day like Swiss Independence
Every door you closed I have opened
Reality more strong than the traitor's arm
Quite vanquished me

Your hands were blooded bloom
Now the tide hastes out of the view of whims
The sonatas and the caprices unaccompanied
Unaccompanied now and needing no accompaniment

The sluggish window rose
Upon a vista truly opaque:
The view golden but cold, Mother.
Cold Pastoral! Sister.

The sluggish window rose
Upon the inside-outside scene:
So the mind turned to finishing
Excited, near the truth.

With lips upon your back
The pleasure of seeing you
Replaced by the pleasure of not seeing you.
Yet you see me every moment, and momently—

When you see the oak leaf, pierced
In purple and stapled to paper
When you see the brindled grid, and now you see
The house of music splashed with ink.

CONCEALED WORDS

The parts of speech got tangled up
There need be no order and no questions
and no players guessing which quiet game is fun
no map of the world or outline of your face
as memory of you is a bad master
so it's our job to draw you like your France
or my Russia placed in truant space
in alternating colors like bones
Another game played lying down
"Wretch how could you deceive as you deceft
She answered, I promised to cleave and I've cleft"
What tree is often found in ladies' mouths?
What flower do they tread under foot?

They took me to the operating room
and took out my E—energy etc.
We thought of each other as food
Two wrongs as good as a feast
The fairest universe driven to pasture with a blow

You traded proverbs, skipped from instrument to instrument,
Musical instruments like the longest rivers
Scouting for words, for concealed words
I played with the imaginary opponent in the centre
                    of a tracery of lines of colour
Going always in the direction of arrows.

I HAVEN'T

after *See It or Say It in Italian*

"Do you have a lion in your house?
Do you have a serpent in your house?
No fortunately I do not have a lion in my house."

Do you have a woman leaning slightly past the spirals in
    your house?
No I do not have the edge of her dress in my house.
Do you have a lion in your house?

No I do not have the outline of her body in my house.
Do you have a trouvaille in your house?
No fortunately I do not have a lion in my house.

Do you have the goddess Hygeia headless as a house?
No I do not have her right hand casting a shadow on my house.
Do you have a lion in your house?

No I do not have her light peplos folds full of life in my house.
Do you have "truth is the consequences" in your house?
No fortunately I do not have a lion in my house.

What do you have in your high heavy house?
Do you have a rendering of her brilliant pitiless hair falling
            on your house?
Do you have a lion in your house?
No fortunately I do not have a lion in my house.

Rivulet Near the Truth

Sunken rocks are sunless
like a fence in iniquity
or a hedge in oblivion
or sunshine at supper
like the Supreme Being in surgery
restrained by oscillating powers
sweeping the dirty body
useless as if agreeable stuff
like saccharine might look upon
love's clean teeth

Sheep have no tact
at least that one can appreciate
and the playhouse is hidden
like a title on a title page
Today we lie down doing time
listening to Khachaturian's Violin Concerto
a small quantity of music
the guitar the hat the heart
up to the quick and up upon and in with
touched in the wind next to you
traces of a harness like a lattice

in the backyard in space
so we amused ourselves
under true pretences
swimming in leaves bankrupt as Danae
begging in befuddlement
meddling in water in dirty water
excited by mud
fainting with color like Davy Jones
dancing on the back step
upon nothing on war dances
St Vitus attended us
the dove splashing and then
immersed us with a blow
launched into lightness

Sophocles had not written his *Aeschyleia* yet

There are two kinds of sleep
orthodox and paradoxical
During orthodox there are no dreams
but normal diplomatic relations
like a sentence made up to include
the sleepers of the whole alphabet
all the tired out explanations
actually a hole in the ground
concealing a sniper with a sound
of spiders coasting on a rubber ocean
constantly infusing poison in the fly
with the kiss a mother reserves for
a violent child a silk of shiny metal

After an hour of that kiss
paradoxical sleep begins
and it lasts ten minutes
before orthodox is resumed

I believe that orthodox
sleep (the big changes, playing many parts,
silence dissolved by a file)
serves a function and that paradoxical
sleep (a micro-chip and micro-
instabilities) is important, too

But we are alive another way

The vista out this window makes
a plea in a vague style
pale as a persian blind
giggling like refined gold
tempted to please like a pill: Look
The loophole is opening now
looming like a looking glass
the thirsty soul examines
itself and we each other
As it is said you hug
a belief as the playhouse is hidden

Stay Stay Stay Stay

It is snowing on the kindergarten
It is snowing on your eyelids

Love's dice
Are manias and fights
Anacreon writes
You are standing on my eyelids
And your hair
Is in my hair
As Paul Eluard
Says elsewhere
And what do you say? I say

Stay stay
stay stay
streak intrinsicality

An Afternoon with a Lion

after *Learning New Testament Greek*

Towards the lion and up to the lion:
First you were too dazed to gaze into the lion,
Around the lion and with the lion.

Hand over hand you were getting into the lion,
Sniffing palm trees and floating upon the lion
Towards the lion and up to the lion.

In the seventh frame you slipped above the lion
Into the white sky beyond each lion,
Around the lion and with the lion.

Now under the lion, smiling under the lion
It's a light green day edges toward the lion,
Towards the lion and up to the lion.

But how is one to get out of the lion,
One's hat and stick sticking out of the lion,
Around the lion and with the lion?

You ran away from the lion and away from the lion—
Amazed and apart, days away from the lion—
Towards the lion and up to the lion,
Around the lion and with the lion.

Snow at Night

after "Einstein"

When they took Albert Einstein home
He put on some casual clothes and took a walk
They gave him the ice-cream special
       called "The Balt"
             The violinists were leaving but not rapidly
             They remind me of time Albert said
             Always going but never gone
             But it's only eleven o'clock I said
Albert pointed to the cone thumb first, then to himself
Einstein and I nibbled our ice-cream cones
We looked out the window and said nothing
Both of us finished our cones at the same instant
             Under a lamp he gave a student his umbrella
             The snowflake kept falling on the notebook
In Los Angeles now
Einstein felt the earth shake under his foot

The second fiddler was Queen Elizabeth
Tea under the chestnuts, and a walk through the grounds
             Passing on the king's regrets for
              being away
        Adding, You came down from your peak of knowledge
        And gave me a shiny glimpse
Einstein finished his ice-cream and handed the waitress some money
The waitress gave him his change over the counter
             She thought about the tip
The ice cream and the snowflakes and the earthquakes
  It didn't work out and he didn't like it
He had put the knife in someone else's hand
It was very hard and he hated it

The Devil's Trill Sonata

I

As Aeschylus puts it
in Frag. 351: Let us say what comes to our lips, whatever it
may be; or perhaps, Let's say what's on
the tip of our tongue.
    As Achilles put it to Apollo,
You have made a fool of me.

It was with some interest
I noticed the violin back in its case
of itself, was playing the piece
correctly and with almost
no trepidation of the string!
It played along and is playing
by and of and for itself—

And that was the end of our friend
The wisest and best on this earth lightly inclined—
"Be mute for me,
contemplative violin."

You clamp the rifle and release the bullet
And you know that it will always reach the target
And the ferryboat sails straight across the river:
It feels normal in the still air.

What course must the aviator set
On a level road when the day is wet?
The tracks of the raindrops on the window
Are dropped from the bridge by a boy.

You place a smooth box down like a stone
And you rest on your own inclined plane.
A stone is seen to pass through the window
But now the stone is snow.

We have so few red flowers
The stem hangs over the edge of the table
The flower leaves the stem like an aviator
Or like the man in the elevator.

The milkweed fills the sky
Which is small, pale blue, and almost white
Like the game lit up at night.
"We have reached the bottom, you and I."

Half-divine, half-raw, half-German, half-Greek
Time now for an excursus to the centre of all this muddy junk
I gaze into the hilarious sky where flowers gather unknowingly
The last row in a theatre of stars

Dear cloud, free from moral guilt
I see you dragged like a heap of small sacrificial cakes or
                              swerve
Streets tarry in one place, and satirical teeth bite and corrode
Stinging clouds are worse

Oh clouds I fall fighting against the whole Persian army
A pond's another place where streetlights delight to roll
                              in gewgaws and larvae
Andromeda, make steady my steps
You who had but lately begun to exist, who existed formerly

The sun is hot and scalds the little day.
The plane sails up, stalls slightly, drops its nose in a dive
Into a barrel of dimes.
What tree always has a partner?

What flower do most people go far to avoid?
You are beginning to find a bed very boring
Yet you are not allowed to sit up more than an hour at a time.
Mother stands straight up at Green's Five and Ten Cent store.

A supply of white floating soap, and you are all ready to carve up
This tray holds all I need;
It's a nice clean occupation.
But I am not sure what these incalculable beasts may do.

You need a ticket of admission to my rooms.
Naomi and I make up contrite items and float them down the stairs.
You are lying on your back in the honeysuckles—choking.
My entire life was being decided by five nincompoops.

Father says, I will get you a glass of water
If you will bring me a leaf from the linden.
So you ran to the linden tree, crying Dear linden, dear linden,
Give me one of your leaves.

We must keep this heat.
That is we let our clothes get cold instead of ourselves.
Three shirts are warmer than the whole out-of-doors
And the soft inside part of the house. Because we are
          half air ourselves.

What is the difference between a cloud and a spanked boy?
Dear Sky, we who are about to slide (on ice) salute you.
I take my snowy map and look at one country for three minutes
Only a minute to go; that's not asking much of your memory.

Up goes the curtain; Columbus discovers America.
In this story your hands play the part of empty barns.
Up goes the curtain; Cornwallis surrenders at Yorktown.
You open your hand to show the five sheep sleeping safely
          under the tree, which ladies wear around
          their neck.

The horizon is an accumulation of dissolved sky materials
And the sky is an illustration: for example, you appear
As a diagram would make you clear or attractive.
A cloud leaps from one place to another, wishing ill to enter.

One horizon is strikingly like a shady tree,
But inferior and has no sweet or edible fruit
          for the mind's imago.
All insects are illiterate, and your mistake also
Is marked by the immeasurable crudity of your shroud of a
          parachute.

As you begin to shred it, the lateral support from the clouds
Lifts and contracts your shoulders, and you fall
Through an indifferent or averse heaven to end covered with shrubs
Resembling a shrub actually, and shucking off your little
          wrinkled skirt in the sword grass.

This picture of you consists predominantly of wingless insects
Hurtling through the air on superficial wounds,
Finally adhering to certain showily blotched flowers
Where the gradient was so gentle the blue current was invisible.

The gradient is so gentle the current is invisible.
If twilight is a state of imperfect clarity
Then this is a period in decline. Like the bare leg of
          a cautious business man on a polar night
Regarded as a kind of gratuitous addition.

There we are, like two crystals grown together
In a specific rational manner, twin city in full night
With set arias and binoculars adapted for use at the opera,
And you so silky stretched over and under me like a steel frame.

In the dim light, a romantic mollusk closes his shells
And the bodily process suggests a lid. Ophelia green
                    like so many mottled rocks
Drifts with her kin in an area without trees:
Two pages face one another in a book.

Mouth widely open,
The heart-shaped heart, strung typically with one string,
And now scattered under mature trees in sheet from pig iron
In a planned series of moves as at the beginning of the world.

Book with no cover or with a flush paper cover
Urging us to do something and attacking one's past
Rotating the television camera like the Greek god of the forests:
You alone lack the implication of any previous activity or
                    agitation.

You are calm in the following strife and archaic heat
And the children stay behind with a little French.
The fool had to be tricked to finish her dinner by then,
But we two cherished our certain defeat. The rain shot down
                    in an especially casual manner.

And the snow began to plink at random targets,
As if the earth were a plotting board,
And moving like someone dropping in water, you fell
Under the dim umbrella's stained umber.

In the clear and putrid water, like a necklace of gobs
Floating and dividing, dividing and growing, clinging,
The basis of your earth is wet and clings to the wet:
Muddy valves, in air and trees, muddy food.

The reindeer walk by the running water.
All week we were attracted to some point.
Like animals that are food for human beings, world-wide lichen
                    and air on occasion filled with balls and
                    sexual spores
You brought yourself into water, into darkness, into quiet water.

In July we broke like strings, swimming in sea lettuce.
And now like specimens too old to be allowed to dry
Before mounting, merely floated onto the business paper
To which we will finally fasten ourselves and adhere,
             under pressure

Like brown shoelaces, growing in bed or in the garden
Common as stones and shells, held erect by the air
And reaching you by summer and there rot, not easily seen.
When you died, a harmless bird was permitted to
             disappear from our sky.

Little is known, but spiders are found in birds' stomachs
And rats have taken to living in trees, in mongoose country;
Jacob sent pistachio nuts into Egypt; a hot summer day;
You see my white shadow on the wall, it's Caspar the
             friendly Ghost.

Never again to trust the sea for delicate spots
And so we sink, diving and dabbling where you go
And doctors float by on hands in the burnt umber sands
And you faint murmuring of the terrible somersaults of shells.

Bad likeness. We climbed to the highest available point
With your perfume of sick whales
With your ninety foot wives and their eighty-nine foot guys
All opening their mouths, slothfully clinging to twig and leaves.

Twigs as well as leaves we were tolerant of each other.
Suddenly the heal-all had a height of two feet
Many found themselves stuck in duplication of time
As well as instants of music, simple flower.

"Thimble flower" and you too smooth and finely fuzzy.
In the night kidney-shaped and grey
The telephone crowds massed through the turnstile
On way to the voting machine:

Infamy lay on your lips and nightly teeth
Your hands pointed out the seven seas
Dusk opening and remaining open until morning
Branched and unbranched and had its poisonous effects.

Pilots file by, in air, but the mountain is shrewd and
             circumvents them.
In the dim Italian operation room

As the doctors dance this dialogue is spoken: Gastrula,
                bastula,
This music is continuous, as you intertwist and vessels
                are cut in two by sailors, doctors.

One relates to this to the point of frenzy, which it hates.
The children stay on their seesaws, in underwear and their
                outer clothing.
But the ground is slowly oozing out of the park
As Mae West was noted for herself and inflatable life jackets.

        In the earth departed souls slide by
                In a world of organised crime below the level of ordinary
                life
Their colors seen through waves and forfeited land,
Beach that failed to appreciate the risks involved.

With a message in code: Returning from abroad.
The harvest is soft, the beach white, and your breath is assent.
Wiser the nobody, the father to the thought,
The wind deviating as a bee joins a few excluded plants.

I should eagerly like to know anything.
To limit my statement to an ascending climax
Let you take advantage of this googol of forget-me-nots
Like that big blue bumblebee drawing himself up for a speech:

Come unto me all ye who labor and are heavy laden
To prepare for the Flower-Exam, and failing
                twice, become a whole ghost of pollen
To be on the way in the wind
The skin all dressed up, apples brewing, odors
                looming, and events winding into fermentation.

Next you write the girl's name, fold over,
                and pass along.
Then the sentence where we met, prepared for whatever
                might happen like the pavement.
Next what you did; what I did; what you said;
What I said; the consequence; what the world said.

I said, Do give me a kiss, whatever may happen.
You dusted off my coat. I hit you with a million dollars
                worth of mislaid gold.

So you decided to dive into these weeping clouds,
              tackling them without difficulty.
The world said, "That's what they said."

Amusing resident of rooms in which we live,
I remember you when every tree was filled with you.
Now the fool is parted from his lasso
Harmless pleasures a thimbleful of fluid might erase.

Tooting in the miasma, along the serrated edges.
You lie in wait, in the throat of the flower.
The slow ones and I stay behind, obeying death.
The slower ones stay on a single flower.

A painful shadow settles on the second violin.
Your hiding places are limited and easily localised.
In the back seat, sprinkled with introductions, we kissed
A sparrow then I built in trash

Because of your delicate nature I stuck to paper
As the heavenly eye closes, the lion reaches climax
The spider jumps and hides in silky nests
Now disentangled we abscind in snips and fritter away our trips

A woman showed her nipples on TV
And inserted a syringe injecting milk
Into her slightly swinging breasts.
And a lovelier woman bent her head to suck.

The shirt of Dejanira flaps in the air, streaming.
And you stretched out on the bed, enigma and reward.
Or we who embraced flap loose from head to foot.
You have done nothing but try to stand on your hands
              for ten seconds

To win the one way out of a sad course.
But it is not nothing: the tuneful music, little elegant doubts.
Tabula rasa is no joke.
They killed Niobe. *Cartaga delenda est.*

Oh bees one pound of your honey represents twenty thousand trips
Each trip a mile, and every individual must die
The fragrant flowers shudder when you give your extreme sting
But these plants are not easily affected by our thoughts

My thoughts easily affected by the frosts and draughts
Thoughts in the muggy swamp air flash
"Like a match held near this orange flower
When the snowflake falls on the toothache tree"

Angelica is stripped to her smooth bare skin a common complaint
Fortunate to wake with her question seeming part of it all
What is the difference between sterile and fecund?
What is a dome? What does Chant d'amour mean?

We would sail away in this big conversation
Take it in our heads to go into the financial purse together
Find only empty islands so our tears would patter on rivers
            like tins of kerosene
And when I saw you I would gobble up rivers, matchboxes and all.

When you are asleep I will appear and do that some more
And pass the winter like Caesar in Gaul
So I race after you but you put up the storm windows
I lie in bed like the happy book in the library,
            in spite of poverty and pain.

And one day a dry wind blows fractions of a postcard at my feet
The wind that likes to whisk you out of bed
And cover all the space it can reach, swerving
Carefully away, into the black like the balls in the tennis court.

There was no lead in the lead pencil.
There is no bone in whalebone.
In bed your tissue-balloons exploded and Louisa May Alcott
            and the long-hoarded dimes
And you came to give orders to your devoted subjects,
            who shivered into pieces.

This was our game for the old pack of opponents
And it could be played flat on your back.
You twirled the old cards and aimed right for my head
You advised me to draw the lines lightly, so they could be
            easily erased.

Now I see your pictures of a goose presence and rabbit identity.
Each of those creatures must be and is threatened with
            insanity.
Dropping to your knees, you protected my old mirror
            from the lunging air
In it, your own face was white, like candles on the Christmas tree.

When we were tired out we fell among fishermen
You and I swore on sunny seaweed that this penny would be
eternally hidden under the rocks
You enjoyed the quietness of the raindrops falling into pans.
Each drop has vengeance in it. We sat all night
speculating on the baleful spray.

We floated on the big bed like crystal madness.
You liked the flights of those lost pencils all right
Now we will overlap like the ancients with their chains
Shaking them each day, as they are tightened more strongly.

And the fountain ran on, step by step freely falling
And we loved the swath of the evening
You against the balustrade of detested tin
And I leaned against the riddled curtain of your breast.

You hid beneath the grillework roses with a hundred fears.
You suggested to your little patient that I judge the
height of these roses.
You tore and tore and buried your teeth in me, but
I couldn't let go.
Under the rainy rainbow we would lie and struggle like sparks.

Wild coca-cola is easy to find
My own humble lot resembles that of a broken pill
To which I've soared on wings of song
Floating into the land of mystical peaches

My architecture aged one being ruined
Like so much ordinary rice, white! China's greatest architect!
That repeating erector rubber band rifle
Nearly blinded my best friend from the top of the stairs

Botanists behave idiosyncratically outside the Park
The furry elm-tree has moved further away
But when the tiny dragonfly attempts the Atlantic Ocean
Who will be able to force it from that far?

Hand in hand we fled the plain-clothes policeman
What good do parents by smiting their drums
Through thousands of miles of white papers
I direct my happy gaze to the television. A quarter of a
century ago you were one

Like ordinary white rice, rice! China's youngest poet!
And we filled up their bed, Judy, Naomi, and I
And you had to pull it out of closets and look down
            the dumbwaiter corridor
Your face wet with ink

Medea found Jason;
Penthisilea stunned Achilles;
Omphale held Hercules, and Semiramis led a whole country.
Two boys lie under the Empire State Building, naked and crushed.

Only the day is a surprise; the clouds consist entirely
            of ice-crystals.
Why should the old bride keep her distance?
Only the day is a surprise.
As they plunge through her she is heated by friction
            to incandescence

And they leave the old bride in luminous streaks
Before she disintegrates completely,
Falls back into bed with the explosive force of a meteorite.
I approach your metal mouth, you put it near me.

Oh silk that supports the world
That shakes the delicate sun and seals light in paper bags
Brushed up or burnt up or wandering or trapped
The tree is girdled round by disintegrating bark. The pencil
            sharpener filled with a heavy object with a
            need to be turned.

In the other world, in the beginning of polychrome
By the sun's lid, the mule goes down to the ocean
            and the girl throws away her shoes
In your own boat you wait to ferry across some dead young woman,
Who has no boat.

I heard you were draughting pyramids
In the land of wild coca-cola
The days of our days together are filled with sour plums
This whole muddy May has ruined my white suit

It's as if we were at the fingerboard, the keyboard together
And my throat were being torn by a crying gibbon
Whose voice could be heard throughout Washington
Crying, Liar! liar! I have something to say to you all!
            Come to the eastern mirage-tower at once!

Next week I shall sail down on toy boats with physicists
Going as far as physicists can go, looking for you
The thought one couldn't buy you has shattered this
            homemade mirror moon
That is the white suit, which has flown into the sky

Your heart-shaped boat was dragged through the air
Your stream-lined body moved into the stream
In this room, you are only a drop of blood, Science says
And you have just completed your tour of my heart

There are worlds above us, too;
The inhabitants of Jupiter don't use psychoanalysis,
            which they call The Shadows.
Those of Mercury object to the expression of ideas by voice.
Too material, and they have a language of the eye;

Saturnians are tormented by depression.
Moon people, small as four year olds, speak from the stomach
            and crawl around;
Venusians are gigantic but gaga and live by robbery.
Part of Venus, however, is inhabited

By beings of great gentleness, like you and me
Who live, loving, wrong to set foot on the earth.
Part of Venus, however, is inhabited
By those with remarkable red lips and brown eyebrows and
            the diaphanous joints of a crab:

Light brown at the heart, shaded to green,
            and cut into many delicate teeth.
There is intelligence in paradise. Musicians practise
            in sublimity. Only in the music is there
            the slightest crisis.
The leg worships neutrally. The eye signals from a height,
            and the hip moves locked like a dove.

The boar that killed Adonis
Snuffled around the bushes in the backyard.
While two celli played their parts in the trio, a house
            was raised in accompaniment on concrete pilotis:
Inside, music, and outside "frozen music."

She had reduced her methodology to zero.
The ferry-colored stars—stars the color of the Staten
            Island Ferry—

Were strong defiant instruments in glass
Rather like sunlight in a cup.

Swarming with opaque veins into its chair, and clucking,
The air mail envelope hid in a cloud.
You feel that you belong to an era of evergreen trees and
                flying reptiles, not this one
Strapped to the deep-rooted and luminous Dog Star.

You had taken a small sip of a continuous flow
Like a hobby a child pretends to hide
Locking doors and resting after a squabble seemed to sever forever
Relations, as a ship suspected of carrying disease
                is forbidden the shore.

II

Lightly you touch me
paper on which I write
Problems have turned into snow at night
like a little car abandoned in the midst of vague terror

The Bobbsey Twins departed for the depot
Ready for Marat and just as ready for Tiberius
What was the purpose of this journey to Moscow?
I do not think it was clear to themselves

I am closest to you, Earth
and you a pale steel-blue
Life captive in snowbanks
protecting a mouse from a hawk

Like a sex organ on a bright green mat
you favored the cool streams
but you were merely a moss.
Our house a bulky mass of grass, feathers and trash,
                tucked into a high rise

Under a quarrelsome tree of blue sky
We were flying seventeen miles an hour among the poplars
Phyllis is dead and we keep hearing summer songs
while others are prostrate in weeds in snow.

This moment is gone forever
Like a snowflake on a river

And for emergency mattresses
Man uses Spanish moss

Adults move in zigzags
Not necessarily toward the North
Into darkness or running water
Into quiet water

It should not be completely destroyed
Nor unduly encouraged
Look how the bluejay
Has taken things left idly about!

That night the oak tree was rather blunt
Not a fast grower
It had lived six hundred years
Winky the Dog was snarling back at David

The river with its fine hair
Poured out along that smooth night
"Kettle boats" were borne away in clusters
And women hung from the middle like clever pollinations

And we were seeking
Like honeybees behind the Persian blinds
As the SS Xerxes was interrupted on its green street
Your skin flushed, but I was harmless

We called each other names
like mania, convulsion, loss of sight
We became crazy eating your throat
To bring you to a specified state by sobbing
          I ordered you to judge me fairly

I liked the Runaway Star
The Giant Dumbbell Nebula, Triangulum
The Beehive and Lyra the Lyre
Like a violin in blue white fire.

You have not touched me,
but the injury is as great.
It may be we do not have enough October, November, December.
There is another approach:

Kissed in daringness.
Looked for nearby sea.

Yet to pass beneath these misted trees seems not enough.
Laughing at death as you forget the dream.

III

The earth is another appleseed
And you a poppy seed in the parking lot,
        half a mile away
We shrink away from the sun like snow
Setting up the dead men of the day before
        on stakes to terrify the enemy

You dreamt of playing Hamlet our proxy wooer
And ended up instead as Prologue to Troilus and Cressida
Whose love proved stronger than Neptune
Neptune, a pea about a mile away

We went hoping to have all thoughts
Passing through like Christmas boxes
Your own gifts moved ahead
Your brain like a tennis ball somewhere in the stands

You couldn't have had time to talk of the same river
        even once
The football flowed into the centre of the field
But some instant must have been chosen
And we moved along the path dazzled by ice on mica

What was your reaction to your brain on this street
Scratched into the distance you relied only on your knowledge
You thought up a simple reason why we must be correct
Then, like a rocket you looked up

Ophelia preferred to be silk
Rather than inside the glass
The first car hits the second, the second the third,
        and so on
Each whirlpool produces a dimple for Hamlet

Ophelia is some sort of fluid
The silk cloth is rubbed and she flows
Her comparatively small body wades into the stream
She has been rubbed off and migrates into the silk

You make a rough sketch of the swordplay

112 / David Shapiro

And the sword tilts
Hamlet drifts like water through the pipes
The earth is a magnet that can be switched on or off,
        but where is that switch?

We can imagine a film run backwards
Pure milk leaps into the jug
The ashes form a new log
The omelet reconverts into the chicken

The wind which reduces the snowy comedienne
        to a hat
But the hat flies back to the store
The ancient city is frost
And rubble rebuilds in a show of heat

The film didn't deceive you for too long
You saw the joke reforming
On the face of the custard pie
I am of no further use to you

You have used up all available tides by the moon on oceans
Combining in an orchestrated dissatisfaction
Eventually the day is a month
The balloon's buoyant joke is punctured and snow fills
        the whole room with disordered clothes

Lumps of clay collide
And the photograph of Ophelia trails a small bubble
Ophelia still unspent at the end of time
The fountain spouts downward

It was that small fictional dog
That eventually brought us down into the sand
There is only one real Hamlet, but the student
        is advised not to adopt it
Ophelia, there is only one true Ophelia

She hangs from her string
And the pilot cuts it
I hold you between clenched teeth like a trapeze
On the chair in which you were vainly swinging

We had no way of knowing what the insect was knowing
No "love" or "desire" of that mother bird feeding

The worm as it consciously decided to crawl away
We were so close together we gave a single impression
on the photographic plate

Your bundle of human hairs exposed to the atmosphere
The tuning fork kept vibrating
Organ pipes and trumpets were meeting halfway
And blue-green life took place in some of the clouds

An insect walks by along the wooden rule
He is hit head-on by a puff of wind
He is wobbling slightly on the desk
a jerk with innumerable legs
The car travels straight across the highway laughing

We fight but with violin bows
You tickle me into Fiddle Faddle on stage
July Fourth is mounted on the Deal Casino
Your sparkler reaches my heart and travels in a
fiery path upwards

I was only your boy
On this poor but reputable stone staircase
Again you had a brown thorn in your hand
And once more you asked my help in removing it

The Day Star lived on like an epileptic
Think of poor Hermia encountering Lysander
And then all the young people united in proper pairs
I went home and tumbled in vain through the dictionary

Mozart was a boy and the sonata was normal
There are no rules
But there are many songs
Easily heard by putting your ear to the window

Think of the stone staircase at Cnossos
The treads were 18 inches
And the risers 5 and a half inches
Now think of the flight which stood in front of Le Puy

The stairs still exist, nor have they yet been buried
Successive stages of a ziggurat
Leading to another Propylaea
Or sloping corridors of the tireless Sphinx

Elsewhere, in the Chateau of Chambord
Or in the circular tower of Amboise
Or for instance the fallen one of Mark
Stairways of Ireland, wholly embedded in the earth

I a robot and you a robot-ess
Exhibiting all of the symptoms of love
As if a threshing machine
Had come to a farm

I played for you on my resonant box of peculiar strings
four open notes
in the normal pitch
Judy was picking up garbage with a bright green stick

It is a false etymology that has embedded you
in the language and now a false entry to try
            and change you
You began with your desultory raids
A trained soldier is often afraid at sea

You took two music stands and placed two equally distant
            and let a third be farther removed
In a shower of warm music
Your body in the air mail envelope revolved
Chilly in the jet's kidnapped chambers

Kinderszenen
It is a murky firmament in which to shine
This is you, wind
This is your life pushing against unbreakable panes

You were bigger than me
But you were still in the family
As a viola is in the violin family
If pitched a fifth below and empurpled

Summer dusted with pollen
Drew back
And then it pressed up like lips
As we entered the stigmatised cellars

And as we entered the Bogey Man
Edged forward with underwater spearguns
And so the sweet green violet
Was permanently closed

We were natives of Alps
And had the power of reducing all cancerous
                growth
I played you my resonant box of peculiar strings
four open notes.

Unknown woman, unknown physician, unknown Roman
Cut in two by spring vacation
Unknown man, so-called, beside me is a tiny coupon
Eaton's Berkshire Typewriter Paper A 201 and liquid
                eraser fluid:

Shake well, touch on
Blow for instant dry
Retype. Product penetrates.
The rose of the poet and the rose of the botanist are one!

But the specific achievement of America
Expressed in the scar above the temple
In which the bullet is painted, in blonde hair,
Is the unsparing "trans-naturalism," blending both head and bullet

Throwing off rain and snow like a feather
In the attic the child confronts his cardboard toys
                and waves them aside
Reduced to a few projecting ledges
On which my puppet Marcus Aurelius is perched

We note a pure distaste for growing outlines
And underneath the eraser fluid, set off
                against the high lights
And the whole surface thus scotch-taped
A compromise between a bird's eye and a continuous style,
                which cannot be successful

Time for a second coat, where the white ink smeared
Non-toxic and nonflammable
The squat figures of Senators groping for work
An open situation is what the rose prefers

A baby held on to a car
I said, Little baby, do you know where you are
One moment in Italy, the next moment in Greece
I dragged the baby through the window-seats

We passed that store of tiny books
Nancy and Sluggo walked past the park
Their father had antlers, their mother had lamps
And other living room objects on their inky heads

And children passed their calm relations
Calmly dead upon the shore
Shadowed by the rusty bulwark
And women were suddenly bitten in Florence by their dogs

The deluxe circles are empty
On infinitesimal feuilletons
Collaborations between Nancy and Sluggo
End in the living-room, when father puts out the lamps

Several falls of snow, and some sledding
True winter since the seventeenth and hard ice
We have come a long way it is good to be sleeping
Far from our starting point, your voice

Sleep pays, and time is the explanation of a brute
About a bewildering amount of red-eyed space
You I resisted but the poppies provoked me to it
The recovering breath of your sleep-drowned face

A person of doubtful meaning stabs you with a knife
All a-tremble as if circling for a fish
And you are running away precipitately with your life
Wearing the garbs of chivalry, as we kiss.

The dead play the piano.
Without instruments, but not without sounds!
Some prefer *Kinderszenen*.
We are alive, as a maple-leaf!

You notice I don't talk about Pythagoras
I don't even know if there was such a man
If you want to know what's around you
You don't look up a catalogue of appearances

I don't know how much we owe to
Pythagoreans what we call Pythagorean thought
These principles are limits, almost standards
This strained Plato and is lurking in him

Whether it's participation as Plato said
Or imitation as the Pythagoreans said
Plato grew more and more Pythagorean
He met Pythagoras in Southern Sicily

Plato announced a public lecture on the good
According to Aristotle all the people came
Wondering what Plato would say or hide
The lecture contained nothing but numbers

I walk on the dubious roof my father built
Straining to inspect the cracks that will come in my day.
The dog is an honest animal, plain-speaking as fabled
But the pelican eats him anyway, for all of his venom.

This ladder is too short, and does not reach the floor.
Nor will I descend it, though Dad request
Mother is sleepy, unhappy with all these brats
Without whom she is the happy accompanist,
                when the sonata starts

The elevator slips so far, so fast
Surely the ladder then is an improvement
On the elevator in this respect. And don't forget the
                fireman's pole
Or Rapunzel, whose hair was a staircase.

It's nice to have a kaleidoscope in the house.
You stamp your foot in the lagoon, you can't even cross
                the same river once.
Wading placidly and alive, you enjoy your borrowed toys.
You walk out for the Sunday Times and forget to return.

The sun rises above the pitcher's mound, like a mail boat
The stars are now thoroughly scotch-taped
                along the sky
And we lie together like tree-lined streets
The speed-limit sign and the white Volkswagen

The Divine Comedy of a postcard
Living on the earth is like dinner on the ground
The air is filled with warm air and torn pocketbooks
THE President has some other good news:

118 / D a v i d   S h a p i r o

The sky is blank because it's blue
The sky is blank and it is blue, filled with habits,
        filled with habitable houses
Filled with spirits
"But I don't see anything"

It's a bright day in the mail boat
The sun keeps rising out of the mist, large
        and calm
The wind passes the pump house
As if it entertained great scorn of Hell

1973–1974

Lateness

Fraita Shapiro (1920-1975)

The nerves are foolish invisibility induces offers
Tears streaming as if attached to some creed
Are mildly antiseptic due to salt content
Tears secret and stainless
Precursors for the sound of your voice

People burst open and are released and release
    themselves
Easily picked up in that wind
At the lower and rounded end of the "heart"
No man ever saw those forests of fern but I see you
    in your bed
As you floundered in a stream of air and light

Blue and brown and black and hazel
The eye divested of tears like insignias with a blow
The lachrymal apparatus remains and the bright room
We are separate now and move rapidly like tears
The legs from the knees are missing

And the arms are joined awkwardly to the body
A lion tears your hair fallen low at the back
The whole world would have been the pediment
The lion's mane has successive rows of flames
In your missing hand you would have held the lion

My face, the "epigram" is carved in large red letters
Above are holes
Feet of the deceased
And traces are preserved of the wise and excellent
    doctor Aeneas
Doubt is represented and traces of blue wine with
    nine carved petals

Leaves are falling in schematic folds
The tongue of a conquered hero protrudes slightly
The face is long with a battered surface
Inscriptions we engraved on our thighs

120 / D a v i d   S h a p i r o

A leaf falls from your lips and I am in love with
    my lot

Only the upper world is intoxicated
Colour would have covered you
The scene itself comes from some original
The child extends his hand in an eager manner toward
    his mother
In his hand a puppet doll of the deceased

In the hole in her right breast
Would be wedged the spear of the victorious warrior
Only her head is preserved
It turns back in agony
Thus drowns back into the depth of the shrine

It is the work of a good sculptor
It is difficult to distinguish between the living
    and the dead
The deceased plays the piano
In the airy plains of the ocean, a rich throne
    which shows
The need to heroize this woman, unjustly dead

Eros touches her lightly
With the palm of his left hand
The little refugee can scarcely stand on his feet
A young woman is leaning on her arm which, stretched
    vertically,
Closes the composition

TO AN IDEA
(1 9 8 3)

Falling Upwards

A certain violinist had a beautiful violin
But before he had had time to play her long and listen
To her tones as such, he was compelled to renounce music
And sell her, and go on a far journey, and leave his violin
    in the hands of the violin case.

What was there to do? It is said You cannot live life in
    quarter tones.
What was there to do? It is said you cannot live your life
    in silence.
What was there to do? It is said you cannot live your life
    playing scales.
What was there to do? It is said you cannot live your life
    listening to the Americans.

What was there to do. It is said you cannot live your
    life in your room and not go out.
What was there to do? It is said music disobeys
And reaches the prince's courtyard ever farther than smell
    and grits its notes like teeth and gives us food and drink.
And orders a fire to be lighted, famished silk to hang over it
    and repetitions to be sharpened.

What was there to do? It is said it is the violinists who
    do not sleep.
What was there to do? It is said we think and don't think;
    we are asleep.
What was there to do? It is said music sinks into the mire up
    to its neck, wants to crawl out, but cannot.
What was there to do? It is said the violin was a swan,
    seized the boy, falling upwards to some height above the earth.

Unwritten

1

On the border of the illusion
Phaedo condemned the death of Socrates
But in so doing he missed a single day
And rendered his own judgment like an entertained
    breeze
It was a jailer who introduced us
He was a jailer with no appetite
And you know how fire is delivered
By children frittering it away in frozen speech
Men call this pleasure like a place of rapport
But it—is it bliss to juggle the body
Like a house with great pain persuaded to stand
The swans change a lot before they discover
    gods they serve
He sat on his bed and had time to say a big thing
The wind ascending at the corners of the
    cardboard world

2

On the border of the illusion
Socrates and Phaedrus made a shimmering detour
They pleased themselves in their descent
On the border of the illusion where they
    reassembled the cut sentences
Phaedrus applauded the truth of leaving
But today my shoes are all worn out
Socrates said I want you very much
But try to find another time to sit together
Phaedrus was the pleased student shadow and fresh
    air
Socrates was going to the young rhythm
I want to repay this very good but tell me
Do you believe in this fabulous affair
It is he, it is me, it is charm in lieu of sleep
I am surrounded by the summer you sent me,
    your throat on this stained floor

3

On the border of the illusion (at the very edge)
Socrates said Let's go Crito obsess yourselves
You were a slave with tender hands and dwindled too
Sometimes we'll come back and give out poison
Now it's all boiled up and just as ready
One likes to drink and walk and having drunk
You feel those heavy weights like a dog
The lips of Socrates were very peaceful then
You had your lips next to me drinking and having drunk
You covered up your closest friends with a mind
It was cut like sails with the same razor
It was ice and radiant touching to be him
Now we owe a rooster to forget it would be impossible
In a convulsive movement time says time and closes your
    eyes

To an Idea

I wanted to start *Ex Nihilo*
I mean as a review of sorts.
It's too much of a burst for some,
Too unanalyzably simple for others,
As one called perspective that vicious
Doctrine, but is it: to know nothing,
To taste something, dazzled by absence,
By your chair, by the chair of Salome?
Or yet another familiar dedication:
To an idea, writ in water,
To wild flesh, on the surface alone.
To you who carried me like mail
From one house to another.
Now the cars go past the lake, as if copying could exist.
The signs shine, through the Venetian blinds.

To Industry

I took a sewer tour of America
With Jean Valjean a comic older poet
His poem was tunnels
And mine the inability to follow.

Vade retro mimesis. He cried
And mimesis followed (a mime).
Vade retro, mimesis!
Vade retro, mimesis, to profile, frontality, and back.

What I could do was rise up out of the tunnel
like a bird and as a bird
delightfully above that poet-bird's head
enjoy my feathers despite the fears of height

And definitely exceed in verticality
what I had lost in horizontal fight
And like a scarlet tanager I fell
and was kicked out on the earth as a man
    as an idea

An Exercise in Futility

I met an university professor in an antique land
Who said: In my hand is a cartographer's dream,
The country which blurred genres.
                    To release its secret of release

Under the cartons of cardboard script, the discoverers, the learners
And one's own fingers exploring the dumb thick maps.
Oh secret love, heterodoxy, self-deceit,
You have reckoned without the host and taken the shadow for
        credulity
And dreamt all the rapports, at the foot of the airmail letter.
The nicety of a hair, the pleasures of exit
Writhing in passages,
Alive to the needle, down clever arches, hunting you like a bluejay.

You whom I had loved for years like a monumental door leading to
An exterior interior: to get to this door you climbed a tiny, tinny
        podium
And there two mirrors poured into each other
In a maroon room covered up with dust of bricks and books:
But for you the mirrors rushing into each other had lost something.

I saw he had no temperament to speak of—
A fan instead of a typewriter; a tree that was watery air
Buoying the bright horizon; three other countries rolled up beside
        him;
And on the other side of him, a picture of him
Where he begs, student-wise, another sage,
For another scheme, like a part of the bending tree
Of desire. The beaks surround him
Surround us and lunge out of us like a wish.

Snowflakes bewildered the upper edge of things.
The bridge is not an argument,
Nor is it a bridge, in a sense.
The birds are flying buttresses.
No impedimenta on the bridge;
No traveller on the boardwalk; two hands are folded above the tree.

S p h i n x   S k i n

In that remotest sky
where the only note is sky
or not at all

needing the mildest comfort
of the hand or not all
or not all again, see

if Zeno is correct we'll never get there

or halfway there

This was to be the hologram of our
love not so whole

in that sky, where all details
begin, begin to be ravaged

mixing with and changing to snow

Here then is nothing but
thought and closures

Two houses embrace
Night disastrous lionized features
    its relapses

So this was the music they rejected
an analysis so poignant it could have
included them
Intemperate or hesitant smiles
and sunny throat
It is understandable if perception
doesn't want us around
It could happen and it did
impenetrable as any door

eyes closed always on the world
The day was your commandment
a work in Latin resisting to have to be everyone
the you Oh to advise things
Ancient activity head and money
as a piano in a clump of chord clusters
ink sun so cloudy a bit Chinese
ink that wanders through Eternity

Forget it just become conscious
think about thinking Just think about it
What you're doing is an umbrella
I'm going to push your face in That's a cliché
Not a ceiling, not a floor
as a sun dwells on a dictation machine

      Ballet stars are sleeping in their shoes
     Hair of your head pressed against hair of my head
Fluttering eyelids of incoming ink
Taking down sentences to freeze the night
Which otherwise might have unlocked itself in secrets
Calculatingly disarmed from the starting point

If I continued to sleep in the right way
     This would become dangerous to the sleeper
The door is not a window:
Don't get between the sleeper and his sleep
Giving birth to reflexes for the writing reader

It was and it was not
My dimensionlessness is
A sycamore that begins in bark and ends in the nude
Ageless bracelets taught me the laws of foreshortening
There is only one *Fieldbook of Natural History*
Only one fairy tale only one Gaius Valerius
Only one facsimile
    There are only two characters:
    the writer and the reader

The shadow of the no is on the no
Maybe the afterimage of the shadow of a no
Do you think if the Erectheum cannot last
then this no will last? No

The Counter-Example

As in Frege's luminous counter-example

Everyone is dead and we will come later in fugue
Or lullaby, according to the mistranslations

Putting ice on the dying woman's lips
Macadam bond is another title

You did not want to paint twisting life in red points
But randomly following the paper, you twisted the lines

Distorted as a man following a dolphin
struggling not to surface but diving to drown

in a drifting wet imperturbability

 The morning star is not the evening star

To the mortal beloved
and to the one of real music

eyes closed always on the world
Poor air, I pull you over me to warm this cold light

But what is closure when we are so open
And what is lack of closure when we are so close

Commentary Text Commentary Text Commentary Text

   In the morning, the water fed the sky,
Eyes of another material had been inserted and the hair,
               gathered into high strands, more carefully
   arranged.
Two more bodies were discovered in the Spanish
forest fire.
Sky like sand, sand like a body
Sun like a breast one faintly outlined
In blue magic marker and bleeding into the margin
Of its own sunny space.

And a stable bridge linking us no longer
August like autumn and the new encyclopedia
Nom de guerre: Nothing.

Nonobservance, nonappearance, noncompletion.

Like the bright male cardinal on the red maple

No man's land and no mistake. No wonder.
Noah's ark nocturne.
Inferno black Purgatorio matte grey Paradise is almost white
Present I flee you
Absent I have you
Your name like landscape written across the middle of the page

House

In extreme pain
Q meets T
They walk into a house
And later a double exposure is sent to S

Somewhere behind the curtains
Uncertainty is laughing
As you ask the yes or no questions
I am moving towards you by analogy

An Early Egyptian Ship

1

In ancient Egypt, when a king died
Details were placed inside a boat
To travel the sunny wake of the Underworld
These grew slender and parted the eye
Slit where the lines show and paint the men
Glued like an exact likeness you do not know
Punched like a pinhole in a bending breeze
As sailors say slitting the discerning tree
Between the fingers and then looking
Go, into a hole of space already occupied
Like the skeleton at the party with a
"Skeleton story" and filled in with the
Blank round of adjectives — It is enough
To show how the skeleton ship might be spun along

2

In the twelfth dynasty, when kings began to row
They noticed you hanging over the enormous bow
The squirrel speeded along the grounds
As if in proportion to the simple craft
Guests died placed in their nightly tomb like East and West
Now the sail was hung and a single star replaced
      the sky
It is interesting not to know
And in persistence unimproved like time
The blinds grow larger and the junk
Decorated as if to prevent us from parting
I am tied around you to make you small
Are the blanks filled now? The loud product
Is finished and the quiet result each one might bring
My head has been removed, with your own hands

3

All is illustration when an Egyptian ship
Passes by with the kings of Egypt
You noticed her high bow and the inveterate boat
And the distinguished guests oh now too small
The king is dead but not the tiny models
They were complete in every detail
And suppose we had a soul and travelled
That decisive stream and followed in foamy wake
With seashells in our ears beyond the jetty
The scissor has cut the sail and the Nile
We are dropping in the mist who love the snakes
And features of the hull and how to make them
History is complete but not the sailing ship
We are lost, like pen knives and scissors in a breeze

The Index of First Lines

Between thirty and forty
Violinists boast of their violins
Like a magnolia in an old home
In the house one asks, Whose house is this, is it mine

The single cup of a house
The Hudson River is a glorious land
The year is closing with nothing behind the veil
Invisible mites level all plants
Click, click, and always in Chinese, click, click
The Palisades with their extrusion and intrusion
The year was closing with nothing behind the veil

Dear friends, there is no cause and effect
I had a will to serve you
As you swerved in your big car

My father and mother lined the returning streets
Ever since the hour they left me for the walk around the Park

Cygnus the Swan is very close but stuck
Like a bluejay that has lost its oak
The typewriter always in front of my bed
For ten years, it never left the bookshelves
But those high words never reached the shelf

Not too gently now I put in another piece of paper
White as a feather or a rabbit or a cypress
Green as heat, and green as the earth her door
Opening on the white water of woman's form
How quickly it dries
One house on the chessboard

In Holland there is not enough room for a mirror
In the wind—many trees—the boy Mozart was frightened
On the lake he could control his remote bed
The year was closing with nothing behind the veil
Dear friends, there is not much cause and effect

In the new street, the art of floating up
The International Tin Symposium, immeasurable pain
It is no insult to say it is like the index of first lines
In the night when I have not lost my hearing
I hear you, your thoughts that went to fight
Your thoughts in my hand like a zone of flowering paper

In the house one asks, Whose house is this, is it mine
This paper is so empty I keep waking up
Inside I play in my light word

The earth will be more precious to you
Now, as it slips under your feet
One of the words that cannot be used again: crystal towns
In the distant water like architecture in the mountains that might
    reflect
The stain growing in the valley's glass
The snow risen beside the unpainted screen of idle windows

A Song

When a man loves a woman
the words withdraw to the palace
he demands his words and rejoices seeing them neighing
                    into his face
the words in whiteness the words race the hasty words
            stand around and excite their breasts

When a man loves a woman
He wraps his coat of words about his shoulders
Scaled with gold and white mountain words
At the same time he fits for wearing both his word and his world

When a man loves a woman
he seizes the strong word with violence and says trembling
Now Oh word never disappearing
Now the world is present and the maximum Actor wrote you (not
    spoken)

When a man loves a woman
the words preside over the pool and the sounding streams
the king of the sky spits and the nymph grace note
of rivers grace note to my mind you know I have preferred
            you alone to all placed you willingly in a part of
                    my words

    WHEN A MAN LOVES A WOMAN BY PERCY SLEDGE

When a man loves a woman
Hospitals are supplied with beds and clothing
If she is life nearer the front
He is fitted with beds kitchens and dispensaries

When a man
the sick and wounded upon their hands like wagons
He gives his ambulance
he is incapable of keeping up with the troops

When a man
the Indian ambulances are carts drawn by bullocks and mules
Very strongly made they are holding two men
lying down and four sitting up alert as a driver

When a man loves a woman
the wounded man is transferred to a hospital ship
in the comfortable swinging cot in the airy ward
and the ice flies into the hot wind and the bed rises on the shore

Yes when a man loves a woman
the bonds of union are drawn considerably closer
In the War however
the present and the past overlap and the skeleton foot of time

WHEN A MAN LOVES A WOMAN BY PERCY SLEDGE

When a man loves a woman by Percy Sledge
he is like a polygonal block of limestone
She is the city and city wall measuring 2½ meters
Two of his gates are still to some extent preserved

When a man loves a woman
Remains can be traced and the traces are finely ruined
Huge blocked halls arise
Two approaches to the citadel added and blocked on the north

When a man loves a woman a genus of the trees
Parts of the world are fruit
Used for good and light
And the man is called the candlenut

When a man loves a woman
she is the vanishing and the lace and the lake
and the seeds contained in the decorated Museo of "of"
The absent town has a picturesque aspect yes

Yes when a man loves a woman
he wants the ruler who would be noble the Swabian line
His nobles whom he tried to cow by sporadic acts of violence
rebelled against him leaving a will and Sancho and Seville and civil
 war

When a man loves a woman

When a man loves a woman
He has fallen by the art of his stepmother
and drawn apart by frightened automobiles
has satisfied his father's hit-and-run punishment

When a man
he has burdened himself with equal arms
to outstrip the wind on an automobile
like a spy approached the camps of the Greeks daring to
          demand the automobile of Achilles

When a man loves a woman
he beholds her far off like a headquarters
first having pursued her through the void
through the long void with a short arrow

When a man loves a woman
he stops his Toyota and leaps from his front seat
and comes up to her half dead with a safety belt
and his neck being pressed with her foot he wrenches
          the wrench from her right hand

And dips it shining in his *alto jugulo* (throat)
When a man loves a woman
moreover he adds these words
You lie stretched out like Italy and the wind shakes her
          hair flying into the opposing comb

When a man loves a woman
each one withdraws into its own space a signal being given
they plant their spears into the ground
and lean upon their shadows then the mothers pour out with zeal

When a man loves a woman
the unarmed populace and the powerless sold men besiege them
the snowy words lie on the oaken typewriter
the black words follow the combs combing out your hair

When a man loves a woman
then the tiger is hungry
and you who composed the songs of shepherds and were audacious
stop singing beneath the terminal the bus station and the goons
                    (cherish me, Naples!)
and the ninth morning displays you homeless as a funeral offering

When a man loves a woman
his neck is untouched and suddenly the words are humming
                    in his carcass like bees
and his dissolved entrails and breaking through the page
and immense clouds of words are drawn out

WHEN A MAN LOVES A WOMAN

When a man loves a woman
he attacks the fleet, which lay concealed
and commands his rejoicing associates to bring fire
and glowing he fills his hand with a burning pain

When a man loves a woman
he knows the sound and trembling flees back
he flies and drives the dark band across the television set
as when a constellation passes over alas cardiologists

When a man loves a woman
they rejoice sprinkled with the blood of his brothers
and exchange their homes and sweet dwelling
and seeking another bed lying beneath another bed

When a man loves a woman
I beg this last favor (pity the seething surface) does she hear
                    any words

142 / David Shapiro

which when she shall have granted to me
I will dismiss her gratified in my words sisters

When a man loves a woman by Percy Sledge

When a man loves a woman
his right hand is torn from his horse and bears him off
and a story is raised then the window shade presses in on him
and the Venetian blinds beat the air with their slats

When a man loves a woman
grapes increase hair and spontaneous flourishes elsewhere
but the stones are established in the empty globe
whence woman a hardy race was produced

When a man loves a woman
the prospect may feed the hungry mind but the land will not give
also you will ask what depth the trenches
Do not commit the vine even to the light furrow the earth is low

When a man loves a woman
it sinks its roots into the Hall
and for many years strong arms and branches move this way and that
Nor let your yard incline not plant the lazy hazel among the vines
                    nor break the twigs (love the earth)

Venetian Blinds

I have been leading the new life away from you.
Or, I have been leading the new life, but away from you.
If I could I would plagiarize from music, for instance.
Also I would send you pure tones or defend a form or try to live

Or trick and manage you as if you had been asleep.
It is a criticism of life or a criticism of death more exactly.
Whistler and Mallarmé's correspondence has not been translated
But when it is, you will note "my Mallarmé" as an expression.

One might call it tracing a hyacinth, or traces of a hyacinth.
Like traces on a blackboard.
Or tracing the window from a neoclassicism upon a blackboard.
These days that might as well not exist.

Amerikanische Lyrik, orange and red and yellow green.
Blind and sleeping and angry nonimitations, flowers.
I could not draw, so I sketched this soundless one of hopelessness.
Between lives occur lamps.

Snow

At first the snow thawed quietly
and secretly from within.
                         Pasternak

On few days has the dark sky cleared.
                         Po Chü-i

Since I was born in the city of Newark
Moment by moment a very fine snow has been falling.
On very few days has it stopped snowing in my sleep.
The snow has widened till it joins the roofs; elevators sink
Into it; in sleep I build snow fortresses.
The sleep I have slept is also snow—
Snow poisonous as underpainting in Spain—
Snow in the surface as wide as an exile—
Snow in the airplanes that almost touch your face—
I advise you not to paint it.
At the end of the street I hear a snowy song;
Snow birds are lost in Chinese white snow;
In a single night parts of the car have turned to snow;
Another car moves forward for science.
Snow has fallen into the old bottle of eraser fluid.

Friday Night Quartet

I
ST. BARNABAS

My mother said,
All surgeons want to do is surge.
And as one took the staples from her skull
She said, Neurosurgeons are not nice.

Mostly blind and leaning against a wall
She told my father, Irv, you can be replaced
God forbid I should sit where I want to sit,
And what's wrong with this chair pray?

Sitting and crying, she said
This is not Chekhovian
Or Tolstoyan, David.
This is annoying.

Lying on the angiogram cot, strapped down and hot
    and bloody,
My mother said, The worst words in the English language
Are these David—Don't move.
And what do you think the best words are: Here's some water.

My mother said,
I'm not wavery because I have a wall
And I love it—
Walls are convenient because they don't move.

One day I walked with a tube of toothpaste in my hand
And Debbie said What are you doing with the tube of toothpaste
I don't know I forgot to put it down
I noticed a slight look of contempt on Debbie's face

Poor Debbie
It must be awful to have a mother who's not very bright
Who asks you what day it is
As Michael and Noah would say Ech and Yuch

The other day we were expecting a new Maytag
And Willimae who's very bossy said
Oh Mrs. Shapiro the Maytag men are here
Put your wig on! For what? Ridiculous!

146 / David Shapiro

Sometimes Dad grabs my face and points me
In the direction he wants to go
And I say Why do I have to go in that direction
I usually respond, Well, go; he doesn't need me to help him
He's adamant about the direction he wants to go

The worst thing about a cardiovascular accident
Is not being able to walk up steps
I can walk around a room
But I can't walk upstairs

There are things in closets I've put away months ago
And I can't get up there to see them
Just clothes
And I can't get downstairs to the cellar to do the
        wash—a pillowcase full of dirty clothes

And Irv says Oh they're not dirty
But I think they are
And sometimes I ask Irv to put real hot water in the sink
        so I can take a sink bath
And he'll say You just washed

Don't get a cerebral vascular accident
If you can help it
Well maybe a long time ago I would have thought you could eat
        a lot of sweets and die of a high insulin reaction
But I wouldn't advise anyone to do that

Years ago I used to say I'm so lucky
If I want to get out of this thing all I have to do
        is eat one or two sundaes
And I'd have a diabetic coma
No problem

We sit and we listen to a lot of opera
Pavarotti sometimes Bjoerling Martinelli
The best thing I've heard recently is the Mozart quintet
with Heifetz and Piatigorsky and somebody Domingo

And I find myself crying because I never hear
        live music anymore
It's all canned
If you played here
It would be very much alive

Everybody loved my Dad because he laughed at everybody.
He had a magnificent laugh with tears
When comics came to South Africa they'd invite him
To sit in the front row—he'd laugh loudly

It was quite apparent to me that Pop was not laughing AT me.
And I would stand by the open window when I was 5
or 6 and pretend to be *davening*.
And he would laugh and laugh, this little girl who was praying.

My mother said, If you have a beautiful speaking voice
You can count on a beautiful singing voice.
I used to imitate the little boys in his choir. I would give myself
a boy's nasal voice, and he would laugh.

Sleeping in Gideon's twin bed, and John's twin bed,
and Pop was telling me stories in Yiddish
About little tiny people who sleep in rosebuds.
All Pop's stories were about miniatures,
        mice who ate the crumbs or babies who sleep in rosebuds.
Little people
Nice families who had children so tiny they could hardly see them
and how happy they were with these almost unseeable
        people
He loved furniture that was too small for anyone to sit in
And then he would end with his famous two lines
They were famous because I didn't know what they meant,
A shetkl arain a shtekl arois
Di maise iz ois
Stick in, stick out
The story is finished.
It meant I couldn't nag him to tell me more, I was to go to sleep.
In. Out.
He never told me a story without ending it that way, ever.

II
THOSE WHO MUST STAY INDOORS

DESERT MISTLETOE

Wounds in rainy seasons may become badly infected
But you have many days left
Bones, flowers, March days, white days, days
Growing in the window, where you are grown a wandering Jew

Interesting animals seem to leap from nowhere
Give a confusing series of clacking croaks: A good test for hearing
    some do not hear it at all
Mr Frog lives within jumping distance of a permanent pool
All boys and girls should have a chance to learn about sleek snakes

Where ravens work cooperatively in the night
The stars and the maps and the horizons should now be rent
We mean a number of things, but chiefly we refer
To variations in brilliance, groups of stars, lines in the
    maps now dots

As soap and pie and bread are names for happy or unhappy
    combinations
So are the rocks
So-called seas are darker regions
Hands pulling the root out, twisting it easily from the moist ground
                                 the night sky

"Upside-down bird and twirl-around-a-twig describe antics
Apparently liked by those who do not know your name
A visitor and beloved
By those who must stay indoors"

III
ORANGE-COLORED SKY

My mother said,
I couldn't keep my hand off your face,
I was always caressing your chin.
   We used to listen to a television program, you and I,
And the guy sang a song called "Orange-colored Sky"

And his name was George. He'd say GEORGE.
So we wrote a letter to him, and I wrote it for you and I said
I am five years old and a classical musician
    who plays the violin

And I really prefer Bach and Beethoven
But I like the way you sing "Orange-colored Sky"
And he read it out loud to all the people in the audience
And you heard it, and he said, "This is a letter from
    a little boy, David Shapiro, Hopson
    Street, Newark," which got a laugh.

IV

FRIDAY NIGHT QUARTET

When we dead awaken we'll play chamber music Fridays
Even if wrecked sustain freezing death, still satisfied
She made me quiet, she will again
At a spell of longing, beyond boundaries of town—
    dying—urge—spike—bargain-ardor

Silent man takes a repeated test, a second photograph.
Rotten willow you have an abortive stem.
When one studies crime or the prevention of crime,
    the peony has no money
Dear flower, destitute and household god, my enormous
    youth beneath.

The air thirsts for water
And will accept from any object including your human skin.
Your brain upon bursting releases a shower of brilliant
    cartoon stars
Slowly but thoroughly you sucked the honeysuckle.

A war was in progress between the wasp and me!
Stinging me on the knee, it could only laugh and leave.
I know I shouldn't have thrown a music-stand at you
Moved merrily among midgets, slept a lot in humorous trees.

I sat in my room with these borrowed games
Blandly I steered my flanks toward the sea again
That foolish herbarium. But when I tried to pass
    into that vague life
The fish rose up in a transparent bloc against me.

V

FOUNTAIN

Too dizzy, too wavery to weep
puffy, bald, obtunded
blind mostly,
the so-called silent portion of the brain removed—

a believer in walls—"they cannot move" —
my mother was dying in her sleep
like a cloud that has slipped out of place
and rolled down the canvas sky
Dizzy, wavery, asleep,
how could she die?
That night I saw a fountain
inscribed with this advice
"Laugh loudly, love, as my voice laughs in the grey water."

VI
SESTINA

I asked my Mother for a new form
from Paradise. But all I could
see was a slight surface like the
old toy bowling balls that yielded
little answers. Struggling to see
something, I saw a sestina in lines of
color, like magic marker on a lake:

_____
_____
_____
_____
_____
_____

November Twenty-Seventh

My old desire to live

I've built nothing; you are the architect.
You are near me like the sound of an archaic car.
I know that I love the verb not to know.
Do you love it? The distance is like a Chinese garden.
I pluck pomegranates out of the Halloween stores.
Then I keep looking at this phrase like summer hills.
The mountain represents nothing, the mountain air
Represents nothing, but two birds seem bad enough.
In these things there is an immense exile like a surface:
And when we try to stop expressing it, words are successful.

To the Page

The page is not a deep wood
nor is it a wooded ravine
nor is it a log though it is a slight cavity
lined with moss and sometimes the leaves of your hair

The page, the page! The black page too is valuable
The little page swallowed me up
whole and crushed me afterwards
The hours like smoke trees

The page in the Connecticut River
The page in nothern New York
like the moist decaying woods
the page haunted by hillsides and violins and ravines

Oh page I walk about the ground
searching for food and the like
but you have no special interests
scattered rather than concentrated,
        with a secret like that of the sparrow

Thin Snow

Screens in a dream,
grey blinds,
robots toying with a tree's model,
images of images,
worlds, not quite, taking a bath of time today,
your face on the music stand,
sedentary mentalisms,
quotations, dissertation on,
family carving,
travesties—
are torn paper,
doubt like looping wire,
a buried city for color,
the river tears space
the inside of broken chalk,
nothing is behind poetry
though it hollows the page
And so the snow fell
and covered up poetry.

Four Lines

Forced to sing O History
What you need is mimesis
A boy and Psyche once
Came together in a dream

A boy and Psyche once
Came together in a dream
Forced to sing O Mimesis
What you need is history

In a dream David and Psyche
Came together
Forced to sing O History on a bridge
What you need is a bridge

Cupid and Psyche once
Came together in a well
What you need is limitation
"Oh mastery"

I don't mind height if I see
Such ships bridge sky and water
A boy and Psyche once
What you need is imitation O forced to sing

The Night Sky
and to Walter Benjamin

Best to use a dead and nervous language
The extraordinary effort will do nothing
The sun is so close to us
The moon of Pluto even the newspaper's moon of Pluto
so far away
The one thing Hamlet did not mention
is that things might get better
In the clear sea a little glass pulverized for my pleasure
You do your griefwork, dreamwork, like homework
Someone lost his money in the night sky
Someone cut into the shape of dice
threw the dice against unbounded odds
light from falling dice

Name and Addresses

Pythagoras said,
Upon rising from bed

Obliterate the print of your body
Innocent archaeology!

Rats surround us
And we call them squirrels

If they had thinner tails
We'd call them rats

Guilt is longer than love
Longer and stronger than love

Philodendron
And the rats live on

Vibrant disclosure
and deadly closure. Of the door.

Even sleepers
Are workers

And collaborators
Electrons that once loved each other

To the Earth

for Meyer Schapiro

I fell with my father through space
In a space module as round
     as your thumb

My father remarked of the earth
How they had divided everything

By twos or by one (a joke)
It was better by far to visit the other side
     than stay stranded in that self

We passed the poor Americas
     South Africa striped as a zebra
And Russian artists who could not practice their art

The art of the grid
While others wondered whether we had seriously
     judged the grid

But all over the earth the artists painted
     what they wanted
Except where they could not—or what they needed—
     and did not

And my father worried aloud
Knocking on the moonlit plastic module door

When we fell, we screamed
But we were safe in Texas, safe as Texas, safe
     as Texas in Texas

Eating bread not electrons
Madly in love with the earth.

HOUSE (BLOWN APART)

(1988)

House (Blown Apart)

HOUSE (BLOWN APART)

I can see the traces of old work
Embedded in this page, like your bed
Within a bed. My old desire to live!
My new desire to understand material, raw
Material as if you were a house without windows
A red stain. Gold becomes cardboard.
The earth grows rare and cheap as a street.
Higher up a bird of prey affectionate in bright gray
    travels without purpose.
I beg you to speak with a recognizable accent
As the roof bashed in for acoustics
Already moans. What is not a model
Is blown to bits in this mature breeze.
If students visit for signs
Or signatures we would discuss traces.
    We would examine each other for doubts.
Old work we might parody as an homage
Losing after all the very idea of parody.
Traces of this morning's work are embedded in this page.

LIMITS

My father had some curious things to say
About limits, in a dream:
I would not be a curator of the skin
Without knowing the inside of the body.
Think of a general practitioner in Omaha
Keeping up. Think of the optic nerve
Connected to everything, in a sense.
At seventy, one feels seeing and sees feeling.
Then doctor and body crack like a green sea bottle.

THE CUP IN ARCHITECTURE

There is the cup, and there is the broken cup,
And there is trouble in the broken cup.
Or is there trouble with the broken cup?
Is there a collaborative plot, and is there glue?
They have begun repair too soon,
Like details of an eyelid in father's clay,
     Details prepared for a death mask of a city.

It is the cup of a psychotic doctor
On a "talk show" who "acts out"
And puts his feet in the lap of the host
And knocks over the cup without apology.
It is the cup as apology, and the cup without doubts.
It criticizes your work and its simplicity
Because it is evident the cup is finite now
And you had arranged to forget its nomad margins.

In the middle of the country lies a broken university
And there they think of the cup
And its analogies. As the cup to the difficult test
So our broken music and what we think and may
Not think. I ask you to paint the cup
A grave, a cartoon character, and the night sky.
But you have the idea as friend
And certainty is lying there, like a broken cup.
And the lover says Break it, as you broke us.

One has drawn a lozenge in space, shattering
All pastels and later tilting in a more regular
Horizon. You note the archaic horizon
And accuse the present of a lying fold.
Secret waves are breaking: abundance, enigmagram.

I show you the book of Rome: a shriveled
Shell. Embarrassed by pictures,
Clutching at the models like ledges, I ask
Questions about tea: Would you choose

Of the cup, tea or expensive clothes—say
In prison? The laws are insults, insults prisons.
What are you thinking of that is not the broken cup?
We who consume the word, not the elixir.
There must be thirst for the broken cup.

The cup is buried alive, in sand.
The person knocked in the head with wine.
We know or might know now, says the dream,
That such a blow kills the person and keeps
The juices from flowing to the brain.
Nor will children repair it again, like a mother.

You have written in the shape of a house.
Your brother romps in mud outside.
Inside, the sadistic night-calls.
With death a normal life resumes.
The cup lies on the pavement, in stars and stone.

On the road home, you cure a lame old man and give
      him a house.

THE BLANK WALL

"The blank wall is on its way to becoming (sic)
The dominant feature of U.S. downtowns
These are not inadvertent blank walls. These
Walls were meant to be blank." It wasn't a letter,
It was your life; I delivered it in light rain
To the Architectural League. I am amazed at the
Blank wall, it is so expensive, as others
Are amazed that they have brought back the blank wall.
"Oh, the blank wall is so terrible." The grace notes
Strike against it. She is not feeling much,
The blank wall. With beaded bubbles winking on
The blank wall. This happened once to a colossal
Vault of sexual objects in indeterminate cast.
Careless curators, oxymoronically engaged.
The grave stone has a name, it says "Name."
Ah, Hamlet was fat and the jump into the grave
And the temper tantrum, for example,
Will not work. It does not dissolve
The blank or minister to nonangels in the mood
Of sulking brother. Dark, dark, dark, you may
All jump into the dark in a mania of lack
Of doubt. Dark, blank wall, we will stay beside you
And try to learn the lesson without the teacher.
There is nothing behind the blank wall, not even the
      broken cup.

TRACING OF AN EVENING

A man and a woman recite their dreams
In places of fear: a bell tower, behind the blinds, a bridge.
Snow falls on the phonograph
On architecture and poetry.

The prodigal has finished a visit.
The old man was watching from a book.
For so long the narcissus has rotted.
The floor is so far from the earth.

This is where nomads fall upwards
To say nothing in favor of physical pain.
One finds the ocean more transparent,
One finds the ocean more opaque.

A Visit from the Past

On George Washington Bridge.
In negative rain and sleet.
The bridge is fine but not
Its present paltry state.

But one concentrates on a blur:
My book slightly ripped,
Yours not merely human.
All one sees is a photographer.

Mother is burning her father
In layers of newspaper.
In the street it softly falls;
It is a public funeral.

And the critic cries: It is gray!
Yes, but so is grass or your hat.
Like a photograph of hands or a stairway,
criticism could be like love, specific.

She crosses the street to say:
I will be afraid for both of us.
She gives you her laughter: a
rare colorful vase.

Maps of the present fall from me
with exits, entrances, names of the judges, the judged.
Unrecognized, I am so happy.
I shake hands with the past.

TRAUMEREI

One fine day,
open as cut lips,
more than alive—asleep and beaten powerless
you and I
like students evacuating
a burning high school
then lying flat like a drunken one next to the old boiler
in a T-shirt consumed by snow
when us the janitor awakens
we shall be
heated like dead languages after school
safe still, exempt on the illegal floor
in the high observatory
we will pardon the imbeciles
as clear, as intelligible
hardly have time for the brain that kills, bravo
then walking back to school, resolved
under the branches flinging marks
the snow is more than alive, it is asleep
in the little nut-brown street
infamous as sleet as the day repeats
Look at yourself! Look at yourself! That's why
     I'm driving you away
With my infra-red powerful ray
In the absence of a sphere of Lucky Socrates!
Lucky Socrates!
Almost too seriously, and frighteningly, oh sleep.

TAKING A FERRY

Flying onto a ship in heavy fog
Then you appear. Outside, a star.
Some do not look, in fear,
Because we are in outer space,
      a kind of college.

Try to make life something other
Then simply *not unbearable.*
Talk of a show of nomad architects.
Could it be one is trying to
      destroy architecture.

Then go off to build a commodity
And something falls on us like a trick.
Your shirt has been stamped with
      comic strips.
This scene "would be good with music."

You encircle me like a book
As I am reading: A movie of your mother
Nude from the waist up and singing
As a cardboard cutout. Only the voice is preserved.

It's a film of music and threats and mother's breast
Pressed against the glass of a screen.
School? Painting? Oh we are taking a bus
Death says it's ridiculous to give you more time to polish.

A WALL

I have the right not to represent it.

Though every brick is clear as a doubt
Clear as a tear and as a mistranslation
Through the window as through December fourth
The clarity of the facts like light snow
After bad dreams forgotten partly whole
And of the whole a part
One may forget so intently you might write

"I cannot now respond to this abstraction
Unshareable satire, courtly dream, and so forth
Sorry, not sorry" But try as I shall not to bump
Or bash it or lift a camera to a sill
To penetrate a copy or to think I have invented it

A banal impossibility as night is written
In pages splitting into analogies like walls
I see in this quiet sunlit stylization
Holding forth onto a garden enclosed and yet at times
Open in a melancholy necessary morning:

A wall I neither restored nor could destroy.

IN A BLIND GARDEN

The whale
is a room
A light blue room
a blind garden
The skulls make room too
And what is the whale
behind you
It's a complex note
When the whale strains
The little fish die
must die like a school
of lances trained on
our friend of two openings
a blowhole a slippery
prey pointed like a joint
in a design of teeth
Can you guess
which whale
Imagine you are a
whale: what a waste
of captured energy
Jonah sulking
like light in a pyramid

and the summer eats
through you like an
island or like
an island whale
with a huge watery tongue
pushing Jonah to that
elusive depth
where the jaw's
sounds pierce him
ear to ear: it is
fear, fear of the bottom
fear of the crashing filter
of these open mouths
skinning us, squeezing

us and gulping our happy eyes
Jonah stands naked in the
room with no solutions
throwing lots like a blanket

and the whale also drowns
like he/she slightly singing
The first part to break
is the hole tightly closed
Next the subject
Next the streamlined shape
As we are young
we have reached the zero surface
Mother's nipple our first meal
nurses for two years
the richest of all animals
Jonah, grow on this
rich milk
in the unique ribs
collapsing under pressure
like Nineveh of grime
The airplane learns
the song is almost continuous
and the prophet's perfume
is then engraved with a picture
The scratches are filled with soot

In a blind garden
think of the whale
as helping Jonah
a joke in poor taste
in relation to a lack
of consciousness of nonsense
Now think of Nineveh
of madness and associated cities
Dear whale of my youth
you are alive and I am swallowed
Now think of a rotting palm

of a rotting royal palm
under which you dream
of a curse like sperm or teeth
of a continuing city's fine song
that can never be heard
by idiotic ears

the prophet's a skeleton now
what about a coral skull
or a coral penis
or coral without the body
We must blind one another
like pollen in the bright
sun's dust Mercifully
mercy concludes the story
Your dreams are those
of a young architect
You don't want to be seen, but to inspect
the curious architecture
of the island bird's throat
as you grow aware of the
increasing dark green ground
of the truncated future

ARCHAIC TORSOS

after a dream

You must change your life fourteen times.
Change your way of living like writing.
You must change your method and your mind. You
Have to transform life fourteen times. Change life.
It has become necessary to change your life.
You need this change. We need to change your life.
And now you'd better change it: you, yourself.
It's up to you to exchange your life. Change, change!
Alter your life, patch and reshape your life.
"A change come o'er the spirit of your change."
You might shuffle the cards spin wheels change wheels.
You must convert resolve revolutionize your dissolves.
You might change life itself. And you might change.
You must change. You must not outlive your life.

IN MEMORY OF POETRY

In memory of a collection of sculpture, in memory of chains,
Margins, in memory of a concordance of flowers of good, in
      memory
Of the reader over the dice cup, in memory of late human
      shows and earlier
Like a gun in the bottle, in memory of the flowering lady and
      the palace plum, in memory of the masters eroding like
      summer haze,
In memory while the profile of liberty rusts, in memory of the
      green
Journals like a child at the center of the earth, in memory
Of memory not that drawings will stop falling with power
      upon robots
And empire and city, but that small grave steles fall apart,
In memory like ill-beloved winter words.

A Pin's Fee, or Painting With Star

The frame of the world is suddenly rotated
and the change flows through you like a mosaic of diseases
you are sealed off in a room at the bottom, fixed with stars
your earth and your magnet and your little red life

like the desire to cast the image of a woman
on a wall distant as a lamp
a dead body traveling north like an empty house, burning
High above the acanthus
stands the Siren, mourning the outlines
of a spiral

The dead are exceptionally rapt
The hair falls, freely rendered
A work well delineated if cold
Artemis, headless

Recollection sustains a sound
like a music with thorns
You were always softer, always later
in the oblique
like the uncalled-for summer's end

It is as if a clamp had been placed
over the bridge
preventing your voice
not just a sourdine, but the variations of your voice
    your brisk commands

It is a very ancient instrument
the smothered harp
you and I could scarcely sustain
    that first attack
quickly to war but all love studies liberty
and we have hated to hate
like the blue lieutenants and pastel constraints
dwarf mirrors and mirrors for clothes and time poured
    on mirrors of flesh

There is only one secret: the old stylelessness
freedom to visit the fugitives
("You are not a stove. Well, do you mean to insinuate
a person might be a stove")
And in winter we put up storm windows and felt around the
    doors

If there is only one bed
no matter how thick
There is only one air
Two window sashes, one air,
two walls, two shirts, some hollow birds
Black wax: those birds look like houses made of hollow bricks

You already a half ghost
and anyone speaking to you or drawing you even half a ghost
and then you become a whole and drop out of the game
and anyone who is half a ghost and speaks to you
becomes whole and drops out of the game

I am drawing your outline now
by memory
a quiet game which is always a way
and I am trying to place the lakes, rivers
and life's dust within a few miles of where they belong

A BOOK OF GLASS

On the table, a book of glass.
In the book only a few pages with no words
But scratched in a diamond-point pencil to pieces in diagonal
Spirals, light triangles; and a French curve fractures lines to
    elisions.

The last pages are simplest. They can be read backwards and
    thoroughly.
Each page bends a bit like ludicrous plastic.
He who wrote it was very ambitious, fed up, and finished.
He had been teaching the insides and outsides of things

To children, teaching the art of Rembrandt to them.
His two wives were beautiful and Death begins
As a beggar beside them. What is an abstract *persona*?
A painter visits but he prefers to look at perfume in vials.

And I see a book in glass—the words go off
In wild loops without words. I should
Wake and render them! In bed, Mother says each child
Will receive the book of etchings, but the book will be
    incomplete, after all.

But I will make the book of glass.

The Lost Golf Ball

Part of the universe is missing
Sings or says the newspaper, and I believe it.
Even most of it. As tape runs out of a typewriter. Big
    surprise:
And it won't do to go looking for holes
Or changes in the constitution of matter
Like a rare jewel in a crossword puzzle
Or yourself as an answer
Linking and locking up space
In the accidental field where you stumble
Like a star lost on a white ceiling
Parts of the universe are missing
The random minor stars you improvised
Litter the mind but might not go out
Damned to hell not what are you but
Where are you my poem
Nothing is left but the recantation
The repetition in a glut
Miraculous as evil
Joining the democracy of pain as if to improve it
A woman like Venice and like Venetian blinds
Opening and closing
Part of the universe is missing. Missing!

Is this our bedroom or a planetarium?

The title could be an inducement like a lost ball
though it never appears in the final painting
though anything might, a buried ship, the title is a nude
but the title is not a can opener or a handle for a pot
Sometimes what is lost does make an appearance however
taking a common revenge like a word

Losing the lost golf ball, find the lost golf ball
The title itself is a ceiling for
stars that shine at night, will not fade, and stick by themselves
like a slogan
"You have made my room a universe," as you said you would

To Our Critics

I dreamed the dean of architecture taught me how to pitch
With a specific curve
I claimed I knew how to pitch that ball the softball the hard
But he had a specific curve in mind
I forgot my poetry all of it in notebooks like the sketch of a
    glove
Like lost leather gloves without irony to this day
You built a chair for everything
I dreamed I had forgotten proper names and proper nouns
Forgotten parts of bodies like a word
On an obscene blackboard in another dream
I dreamed the critics who deposed the dream had died
Of a brutal phantasmagoria in proscription
They had proscribed themselves

To a Swan

Then you were born, bit by bit, seeing silent and exciting.

You wanted to etch mental pain in the dust.
Then you were born out of buildings and pleasures and
     windows
and the cold painful and colored and fastidious
as a pill in a river: words bitterly little and alive.
Then you were born, swallowing dismissing and rising
Then you were born, angry and artful as a blue white swan.
Then you were born, painting loud appearances.
Then you were born, in the right place like a thumb and a
     tongue.
Then you were born, the animal in detail, impure and good.
Then you were born, breaking up rain ice and information.
Then you were born, fanatic nut to crack a riddle.
Then you were born, nude new and dissimilar.
Then you were born, in a lake like hidden art.
Then you were born, like a baked sculpture.
Then you were born, silent repetitive and good.
Then you were born, swallowing blue-gray and nude.
Then you were born, blind as usual and tempting like a
     tongue.
Then you were born, out of fanatic architecture and repeating
     windows
like art in a lake, like a pill in the rain, as
an angry swan in the cold dust swallows and rises in the cold
     wind.

Untitled

Lord
I have fallen in love with the harp again

vaguely, I saw
that the waves were turning black

it was a friendly ferry

that night you were born

Ordinary Unhappiness

To a Muse

Give me a first line, you who are far away.
The second line will almost write itself.
In times of pain, I open the dictionary.

Like a girl in the last row who will not say
The theoretical part of the dream was herself,
Give me a first lie, you who are far away.

A student laughs: I died once. Red is gray.
Cheat me like a quote, deceiving Elf.
In times of pain, I open the dictionary.

You who tried to carve this family in clay
Skeptical and frivolous as a filthy shelf
Give me another line, you who are far away.

It's a small freedom on a revisionary day
As a jay imitates the human on an elm—
In times of pain, I open the dictionary.

And in ordinary happiness, I open the dictionary.
The words remain, but the guards are gone for help.
Give me a last line, you who are far away.
In times of pain, I open the dictionary.

ORDINARY UNHAPPINESS

Ordinary unhappiness is a long poem.
Long enough. Irregular sonnet. Ordinary happiness: I nailed
    it to the field.
Ordinary, but what was ever ordinary about that wild shining
Object that you hung up like a coat hanger?

Now I see the women in bathing suits wrestling beside a
    margin
Of cool water and they have come to triple somersault
Out of the picture's edge. They want something beside
Unruffled surfaces hiding an enraged helpless *puer aeternus*?

The voice is a wandering part of the body.
I loved you, your lips that destroyed my posture, the snow
That masked the floor. Now I renounce the hysterical floor.

Like paradise or anti-bower or limitless elixir (alleged).
Last shadow of all to be strong as a shadow
Or dance our shadowy weakness as one possible dance dying
    in bed, fortunately.

MR AVERAGE VIEWER

Jerry Lewis once visited my home
Or actually I walked in and found him smoking with a friend
I loved your program Jerry Visits Jerry last night I said
Particularly when you said what you said against the war

Contra deum, Jerry, I cried
My wife didn't but it takes quarts of milk to wet some
(We both come from Newark) I asked him, "Is it true
What they said in Weequahic High about your tormenting
    teachers?"

You mean, he said, the *Cruel Jer*? Yes, I would stand on chairs
And torment them. I told them I did it too, worked with
    children now
Just like Jerry Lewis and his Marathons. You see
I watched those too, I said. You'd like children's works

I recited him one but he didn't seem too pleased.
Suddenly I wondered why I had been selected for this visit
His pal said, You have been picked as Mr Average Viewer.
Now a whole studio crew lounged by, and I prayed
    for you to come home.

DOUBTING THE DOUBTS

A map dropped from my hands
And a voice cried, From now on
You will proceed in darkness.
Alas, he laughed, that is true.

Was it a black map?
I do not remember.

We all love clarity.
But you love darkness.
But darkness is clear.

We do not know now and we will never know.
White night, perilous night.

A LOST POEM BY WHITEHEAD

When Alfred North Whitehead taught poetry at Princeton
He said the critic must not be color-blind, and F. Scott
    Fitzgerald
Heckled him in the back row, crying: All I want from many
    worlds
Is the fantasy of being a fiction. Whitehead wrote it out on the
    blackboard:

"The red world seems gray but it never ends, anti-heroic
"The green world freezes but is a map of other worlds,
    nested, replete
"The purple world connects to all others like a microchip's
    music from a lost key
"And the orange world is not ours to be completed, not ours
    to be abandoned.
    The orange world is also in the orange."

THE BOY WHO LOVED BUBBLES

Because a universe is one bubble
of black bubbles, and yet
a boy is watching always with bloody eyes
—a boy who loves bubbles—
as a black stone rises beside our sleeping head

Tame at the end of a stem
it may not burst like paper
into fifty sheets
as he knows who stripes his notebook with lithographs
Inserting his pen into his mother's black purse
he covers it he discovers it in a glance
with schedules and weeks and a bitten newspaper
But he is looking for writing, the black bubbles

Now what emerges is the antonym
a clipping as colorful and useless as a singularity
and mother's black planet
Now bubble and syllable break in the evening air

You were not really listening to the last sentence
Because you could not see it, the transparent dump we live in
     like a frothy star
Now you are really listening so I will tell you the end

Inside the bubble is another bubble, of course
Inside the stone is a star of pain

Exploding like an accident, the wild syllable, wet
The king delighted by forbidden hair
Poems of birth that were not poems of birth
Music and panic engendered by a prophet without vision
The nostril of an injured monster flaring with a pill

Toby and Nairobi, Thetis the magician
Stigmata on the wand Difficulties of the stateless A cab ride
     wrong
     A ride home Relays
Reading in the dark nothing but the kaleidoscope of the last
     century

AFTER A LOST
ORIGINAL
(1994)

After a Lost Original

AFTER A LOST ORIGINAL

When the translation and the original meet
The doubtful original and the strong mistranslation
The original feels lost like a triple pun
And the translation cries, Without me you are lost
Then be my dream, thin as the definition
Of a trance in a garden
The ambiguous friend responds, Perhaps I do astonish you
Like a boy confused with a butterfly's dream
But you are my dream now, after all
If I don't think of you, you disappear
After which they both comically disappear
Like a slice through two trees for a thousand years
Return knowing coldly a need for guerdons, guardians
Letters written on clouds, snakes on curtains and naked devices
Frighten them no longer since they live only together
Father and son refracted through blue green black moss
They travel together to the margins of a cloud

THE SNOW IS ALIVE

I

The snow is alive

But my son cries

The snow is not alive
The snow cannot speak!
The snow cannot come inside!
You cannot break the snow!

But the snow is alive

And the tree is angry

II

I was afraid into again.
Where can I find you,
Tall flower, redolent
Of the divided spring?

186 / David Shapiro

WALTER BENJAMIN: A LOST POEM

after a dream

In a lost essay on poetry, Walter Benjamin had written, *I was born into a rich, perhaps too-rich and too comfortable existence in Berlin. Each time my family saw soot in the air we wanted to move to another vacation spot. Poetry today withholds too much. What does it withhold. At any rate, eclecticism, Prokofiev . . .* The most Brechtian poem of Benjamin has almost been forgotten. It was published under the title *David*, with a section of a door knob as a slightly Duchampian typographic oddity. I found the proofs, rare as the Redon for *A Throw of the Dice*, in a bookstore. The poem was fairly simple:

> David or King David
> How
> did you
> *done*
> your door

Unfortunately, many of Benjamin's remarks on poetry were now simple scratches on the cover of the book, effaced like the infamous magic writing pad and indecipherable as hidden love (as opposed to open rebuke). Some of his lost short stories appear in this volume. Scholem said, There was nothing like being alone with Walter Benjamin. *It made one want to read.* The source of that remark is also lost.

IN GERMANY

I did not mount Mt. Parnassus
Nor could I walk Philosopher's Walk
    It was too high (*altus*—also reversed)
      Or too late (or—not yet)
I took your way
But halfway there (oh Germany it *was* insane)
   Wanted my own: Narcissus Narcissus
   Then the blue glides off the page

      The beam with its probing lip moved across us
       Recording our model travels

Language in your mouth—fiery as a tongue
Like a flower deleted by a whirling pencil

   We are the sculptors now, making our own doors
   The words remain, but the gods are gone for good

The idea remains, but the words are gone like gods

AFTER ASTURIANA

On the road to a door
On the way to a window

I saw nothing like a soul
Only the dust in competition

Lifted by the air
That was like a sailor joking

Nothing carried to nothing
A sailor was bouncing

In the world's salt: Now dance!
Now you are dancing like the world

Nothing equals nothing like a word
I get lost and make mistakes in your grace

YOU ARE TALL AND THIN

In the circle of the sky
I disembark quietly: You were wrong.

They call this the street
Where a single dove made a difference, where we galloped
over each other like car tires.

The song says, You are tall and thin
like your mother.
In the sentence that follows, you sell
my dirty body.

Does it hurt to mix yourself up with conquistadors
So many hands, so many javelins, so many burials
like the photograph of an error.

Throughout the night, the song thinks
this is it
And often you live like a simulation
shopping for eyes.

I crossed the riddle,
Caring about the colors, water purple and orange.

Plunging like an elevator into an envelope
All these letters, your branches, fragrant Rhada.

While I wake slowly as a child
You are tall and thin on the bed where
you play so well.

You are high and delegate authority
like a lake.
The night dies like a ninny on the wall.

At night you burn like the library of Alexandria.
In the morning you are Alexandria, in a mirror.

You are so black you are white, like a firefly in sunlight.

Prayer for my Son

There is no storm
But the gods are hid
Like a baby
Under an archaic coverlid
The hated father
Like a punitive hill
I am the obstacle
The music of the radioactive wind
Inappropriately hoping
To have prayed
Appropriating the grammar

Of another mind
Have a year in a prayer
A year in an hour
Stars glisten
Outside the window of the tower
The bridge has no scream
Detail it
The architecture of chaos
In the stream
Be a string musician
Battering on a drum
Is like riding
The chances of the sea
The Dalai Lama says Be kind
No maybe
The Russian says Humiliate no one

A friend is better
Than friendship
The Fool speaks the truth
A gun is a false spray
Rats emerge from the sun
In an odd way
Be fastidious as you want but eat
And avoid the contaminated meat

Of governments serving us up
As if we were underdone
Forget what you have earned
Learn to know
What you have not yet learned
Until you confuse the good
With the beautiful
Don't seek out the wise, be wise
Never abandon the beloved
Just close your eyes
To the world and open your eyes

Be concealed
Like a conceptual tree
And when you need to be explicit, be
But watch out for the right cliché

At the wrong moment like the aleatory sound
That hunts you down for an easy chase
Avoid an easy quarrel like a laurel
Stay at the typewriter only to remember
That heaven is a clear place

The Angel of Silesia ought to know
It is not parody you will have loved
Or the hysterical search
To be approved
Other proverbs: Let her be late
And you be on time to beat me up
But without hate
Try to become the prudent imprudent chief
For the oxymoronic sting of a mind
That completely pursues
And presses the redness
Into a leaf
A too cerebral frustrated love's
The worst
By which all late Romantics

Are accursed
So try to see the third coming
My first born
And drink out of the sexual horn
With a low opinion of mad monist mind
That calls false coherence a good
And forgets every color
In the manifold wind
Though anxiety cannot be driven hence
Learn the pleasure
Of poetic radiance
Each artist in each other artist delighting
Opposed to the combat
Of the self-affrighting

Do not be a suicide
Of some professor's self-anointed will
Forget the paternal maternal scowl
Forget the bric-a-brac

Of an infantile howl
Be happy in godless arms
Be happier still
I wanted you, we wanted you only
To be happier in your house
Than those crucified
By the falsely ceremonious
Let pride come upon you unawares
Like a traveller
Who always has the fares
In a pocket without precedent
And even without money
It will be as if you were
That second born
Each note will issue
Clearly from the nonsymbolic horn
You will rest upon her
As if you were a tree.

To My Son

> *King Oedipus has one eye too many, perhaps.*
> HÖLDERLIN

I love you so much
I am going to let you kill me.
Pathos your thin arms your
neck your hair rich
without perfume
and your eyes bright as a brooch
You say you will kill me tomorrow
and I believe you
but for now you must sleep
in my arms like a cheat at cards
Five years we have lived together
counting like the Chinese
I fear every narrow road
on which we will eventually meet
But do not banish me so fast, my son
Your clubfoot that I have pierced
is more beautiful, to me, than your mother's breast.

HOUSE OF THE SECRET

I met the old dead poet
And told him I no longer loved my work
As I had when a child or even fifteen
Sorry I had not written someone else's poem but it was already
    written

He told me, Never think of others or of yourself
Never do anything for others or for yourself
And never write poetry for another or for yourself
Or yourselves

The secret hangs from the top, like a prayer on a branch
It is the house of secrets, narrowing to the last story
Or the house of the secret, singular
And I wept, wondering where he had concealed such bitter sense

The camera was hidden under the floor like a boat
The poem hung from the branch above the silver bridge
Criticism that does not end, even in Paradise
We think it is a bridge because it is silver. It is not a bridge.
Lost is lost.

FOR VICTIMS

They have used the bodies of children
As improvised bridges,
Which they later cross.
First the sun and the moon,
Then the earth comes in.
But they have lost
The atmosphere, which belongs to them

Light passersby

After

There is the gate or the copy of a gate
Blood outlines the gate, like a nude
A pink flower like a tree emits sparks
They gather into a yellow blue fragmentary flower
In the other space, formed by flowers torn apart
It bites the ground, like a blackened moon
Blood outlines a few jagged petals
Where does this flower emerge if not from history
The night-flower beside it is not dark enough with
Turmoil of strokes, with labor **of having been there**
The night-flower explodes, is blue less
Relentless, should there be nothing but shadow
The twentieth century falls off below and fragility
And the kitsch of flowers above, finesse of heaven
No one can enter here, and there is nothing but hope

A Part for the Part

I demur. What was Gomorrah's crime?
Parodying, parodying, parodying?
That grotesque moment when I realize I am flying like a firefly
beneath the frozen, inverted earth
in the shadow of the shadow of a cassette
Oh door to the door

Broken Objects,
Discarded Landscape

A novelist took a vacation with me.
She ate breakfast in my old house like a sister.
She asked me to play chamber music but only for a moment
Then found another way to waste the afternoon alone.

We ignored the immense museum—
Those frightened by space those by nearness walked quickly
    together.
I asked her what she thought of all this work on paper.
Form inhuman form she cried though I begged her to hear a voice
    I was apologizing for my whole life

But the world could not come to a reading.
She pointed to a logical fallacy there the world thick with
Broken objects, discarded landscape.
But I said your face her face was thin with light and weightless.

She was the narrator all right.
But she was also the sacrifice.
Thus if I painted double helixes she would call it
Abstract but I would be painting life itself.

Dido to Aeneas

(after Hart and Osborn)

I.

It was words that detained us, though they do not reach
I was devoted to the future and you like a yellow acanthus
You wanted to bend to some more obvious bed
Sychaeus was abolished after a desuetude
The night also betrayed me but I drew it out
and I asked you many things about very strong Hector
You were my guest and I loved narrative
like an error on the land of all fluctuating seas
And you apostrophized as if from a need
Night rushed down with the stars like analogies
Now when I look up there is only a chaos like a cave
You have become Rome, while I became something like music
You exchanged me for a fate or a work
drinking like long love but I will tell you now nothing

II.

Everyone has been silent but you are attentive
May you have an immense exile like a surface
A god pulled you to my coast in a digression
Everyone wishes to say things even the air
But you have thrown your arms around the image's neck
And escaped alone with your hands: you and I would become the
     same cave
The mountains do they present anything
Nor am I copying you now king of the obsessed doors
I believed you and the equivocations
If only the earth had opened or I could go toward images
I began to speak but I stop in the middle
Alone in the vapid room I could hear you and touch the bed like a
     relic
My towers did not rise, discontinuity equalled the sky,
Day was a cause a name is a screen and we have called it secret
     love

III.
It was the night of tired-out bodies
With a placid sleep giving access to other bodies
The woods are like a sieve and the sky is normal
The stars revolve like lovers in their lapses
Each leaf on the field is quiet like a variegated birth
And the birds in many colors occupy the lakes
Which occupy the fields and the little rough brambles
But the unhappy mind is like a double Thebes on stage
 May our shores combine against your shores
It is possible to hate life and throw it off like a nurse
Oh dear nurse please send me my sister
I have lived and I have finished now I am a big image
I am a city and a statue and a wall and a revenge
It is a recent cut like an accident in a forest

IV.
You always wanted the most favorable time to speak
and I have found the time not to speak
You think you will have names but I follow in sequence
You wanted to see but you cannot even see the cave
But you had to come to Hell and the urns of secret writing
You think you see something and you see the extreme sequitur
This was the last time you said you would address me
By permission and how much you loved permission the word
My eyes can do something else nor do I exist the joke
You are not even interesting as a cliff or a flight into waves
I will hurry away to the one who equals my love
And you will win Aeneas Rome but not Dido
It is not the irresponsible silence of a suicide
But I had the right to the cry without translation

Goofy Plays Second Fiddle
in the Family Quartet

Evil is a proof of God, says Goofy
And I know I'm just a cartoon character
I know I can't write monologues
Like my friend Mickey, But I'm tired
Of being ink, I'm tired of being music
Splashed against trees
And when I go I'll go like leaves into houses
I'll go like color, I'll go
Like my friend Mickey. In a dream
I saw a Dead Street Sign.
My feet seemed tied around my waist.
I was a prisoner of Outer Forces again.

The big crossword puzzle lit up inside;
What is Goofy's first name? But you all know
It was Dippy Dog and then The Goof.
Minnie was a toxicology student,
Because Mickey was toxic. He was so toxic
He stayed in bed all day, like a painter.

   And my friend sang monologues on the phone
   So sweetly, I thought
   I was on an island. But never wake
   He cried and certainly never wake
   Inside a dream and certainly never wake
   Inside a poem.
   You all know my original name,
   But do you know my name now?

You Are The You

You are the you in this poem,
Mon amour.
Harrisburg mon amour.
Boats break.

So-and-so asked me,
To whom does the you in your poem
Refer.
I said, Are you feeling well, So-and-so.

I can't believe I said.
It. So sue me.
I said, It's the beloved, So-and-so.
Oh is that all.

Well, I said, she wouldn't think
It was so little.
To look up into your face
Is like looking into the devastated stars.

Lights of all kinds I traced,
You and you and you and you.
You are the you of this poem, mon amour.
Boats break.

A Dream

Fairfield Porter, 1907–1975

You, me
with moistened lips
we kissed
by the stopwatch
as in the movies
"film time fifteen
minutes"
then my sister on the porch
said Fairfield are you cerebrating
Fairfield came out of the window
("stuck his head out")
and then we began to
question him
He said that the world
after death was wonderful
as the world was wonderful
and that there were no
explanations in this one
just as in a good poem
When I looked for
a piece of paper
it was already titled
"A Family Reunion."

"The Dead Will Not Praise You"

Cantor Berele Chagy

My grandfather emerges
in a synagogue
with familiar accents
unlike his noble voice
a pudgy little man
sweet tenor coloratura flautando
He marches down the aisle
with a blue white crown
Women ask questions
and they are charmed
and he is beloved
like etymology
Is my mother in attendance
or is she dead?
What are questions now?
Are the dead permitted: to
sing? Is he serious?
Are the dead permitted
to return and sing?

202 / David Shapiro

The Boss Poem

—with Daniel

Are you the boss of God?
You are the boss of God?
Nobody is the boss of God
Not me not you
Are the angels the boss of God?
Are you more famous than angels?
God orders himself
To do what he wants
I am the boss of this poem
I wrote it

A Note and Poem by
Joe Ceravolo in a Dream

He was a poet of grammar
and a love poet and what
is more he showed the re-
lationship between grammar
and love. When he perturbed
syntax he seemed to in-
vert? reinvent? universe?
the possibilities of love
by making so many multiple
relations possible and/or
present or present tense.
He is a possibilist poet
entrances with its naive
or Utopian anti-grammar.

    . . .

History and happiness
Are similar:
They happened—
Or are **prone** to happen
Or will happen, burstingly.
Or: they have not happened.
O history o happiness.

Of belief
I love tall, twisted
Juniper
Who twisted them
Like a particle beaten
in a linear accelerator
The wind twisted them.

(What are)
Rocks' birthstones (Daddy)
Birds are the flowers
Of the sky
Bird birds
Like particles hurtling
Through a linear accelerator
O history o happiness.

204 / David Shapiro

The Seasons

Summer
I saw the ruins of poetry,
Of a poetry
Of a parody and it was
Terraces and gardens
A mural bright as candy
With unconcealed light
The ceiling sprayed upon us
With a bit of the Atlantic
Fish leaping about a henotheism
That permits no friend
And leaves us happier
In the sand than in our room
You are not a little bird in the street
Protected by a stationary car
And protesting too little
Synthesize the aqueduct and
The tepidarium and the lion's pit
The sun stapled shut
The sun not a wandering error
Sunspots are hair
Sun from above or in the light's maw
The sun as a windshield and we drove to time's beach
The sun another snowman
A monkey for a child
Unkidnapped calm
Good day! good time! pulverized shore
At night, when everyone is writing
At night, when everyone is reading
Or learning to read in the dark
Time, with its patent pending
Half-eaten fruit of those
Who fear no lions
No weapons
No suspects, no motives
Walking down the beach on
Our heads: man and dog
Forced alike to swim in hurricanes
By the father, actually to dog paddle

Without a subject like a fireweed
Or a thistle
But the law we did not abide and carried by air
A single drop and I mean drop
Of a honeysuckle would satisfy me then
A cricket arises at the bottom of the lawn
Alone and vague it hesitates to mount the curb
A natural fire discovered in the grillework of these woods
The long column of summer days
Scornfully you lower all the eyelids
And we breathe together a long time

Autumn
A project and a lack of derealization
And a warehouse like a button
A facade in dark gray velvet
With strips of false marble lettering
Bending with the remover to remove
Absorbed into the sky like a gourd
My temporary window like a garden
And the stairwell split open
Into the interior view of a sieve
Of stairwells elaborate in cross section
And the axonometric of Charles Lindbergh
A manniquin feted in his aviator clothes
At the Salon of Autumn
With your hands full of women's
Accessories
And the President with his lips
In the frigidaires
And the tires rolling up at the annual
Automobile salon
Something enormous: the real estate
You did not buy
Sunspots bleeding beneath an oak
No floor
No young fate
The history of time-lapse photography

Is falling now
You cannot even take dictation like daughters
You have destroyed a little of everything
How dare you interrupt my house
Of empty pictures
Make music too loud to listen to
Want the bed too low
Don't want this to exist
Want me to become unconscious
Of too many colors
A house to sink
Violins without bridges
Pencils too heavy to be carried
Dictionaries stuck in the ground
And the violin lies on the long black piano and replies

Winter
Hard winter
Unlivable house
Unlivable snow
It is true January
However
My son is smiling in his sleep
After death there are extremes
Of temperature
An automobile is attached to the planet
And it sails the ice like a caravel
It is a word without songs
And one stops on the highway
To observe the snow's perspective
As the executions are executed
With a technical precision
Like Ricci's spiccati
And the dead slide sidewise
While the moon moves outward
Failing to grip the roadway
Like a bed sliding under the frame
Of a cloudless sky

February has clumped and intimated
That I find you in these halls
Of powerlessness
The fields are messier each day
Freezing water throttles the sky
We are idle, like a pair
Of wild cars on the highway
O northern widowed word
Ice like a sidewalk on the river
A difficult year
And the head emits a hot kind of hope
The truth a novel highway going round
The suburbs and ultimately I
Become part of myself not you and a gulf and sea
Held at precise angles to forbid us
Crypto-opponents to join
In natural darkness
Whose tied feet the imaginary rat gnawed through
In comatose sleep I saw you last
No cemetery holds you nor a single
Fire that I could burn
I pretend to approach your metal mouth,
You put it close to me
Brush your lips with ice
In a key he rarely chose the F sharp minor
You used to say Oh you could say anything

Spring
A boy who stayed awake
And what he saw
Very near as opposed to
To the west of everything
He kisses the bug
The charred blossoms of the dogwood
Family sculpture or
Family carving
My father would point to the
Anomalous forsythia

Because of this truthless
Encyclopedism
It is just as good to meet
A dog or a cat
What they left out: Anger
Sex and history
My grandfather died singing
Called the best death
As my father stayed at the music stand
Or the dancer wants to do
That new thing: dancing until the end
A construction site in sunlight
I had written: Superbia's loutish
Psychological best-of-horse show
Does your promise shine like a highway
Like an effaced green work on a wall
Singing and partly singing
I walked with my son a little way
I say good-bye but not enough
He whirls around I disappear
You need the shadow of a child
Like an avalanche
He was glad he had stayed awake
And he stayed awake to this day
You the chrysalis and I the traditional ancestor exploded like
      aluminum

Drawing After Summer
I saw the ruins of poetry, of a poetry
Of a parody and it was a late copy bright as candy.
I approach your mouth, you put it close to me.

By the long column of a summer's day
Like a pair of wild cars on the highway
I saw the ruins of poetry, of a poetry.

The doll within the doll might tell the story
Inside the store: the real estate you could not buy.
I approach your mouth, you put it close to me.

Violin lies on piano and makes reply.
Hunted words. Gathered sentences. Pencils too heavy to carry.
I saw the ruins of poetry, of a poetry.

The history of time-lapse photography
Is a student exercise. Throttle the sky.
I approach your mouth, you put it close to me.

The moon moves outward failing to grip the roadway.
I see you stuck in the ground like a dictionary.
I saw the ruins of poetry, of a poetry.
I approach your mouth, you put it close to me.

A BURNING
INTERIOR
(2 0 0 2)

A Burning Interior

in Memory of John Hejduk

I. BURNING INTERIOR

of a copy of nothing
or more precisely a series
of xerox sketches of
burning interior-exteriors
No one guesses in that rotted century
not nothing but grey hints in
crayon flecks for bitter
perspective produced by a reproductive
machine looking at itself as usual
askance all the black windows blur
into a recessive landscape of
secondaries O like the gate into your flowers
forty-seven tulips shy of counting
then expanding into the scandalous
world since there is one
to die quickly in color in the tub
like Marat smiling and stabbed near the name of art

not Skelton to the Present but the child's future
from skeleton to the President
in this no-place
for any angel's perverb ("the hole in my heart leads to the hole
that is God—which is deeper")
next modulating with words "grey and pink
always work" when the
bedroom doesn't the Tolstoyan hanging
in the sonata of bilingual espressivo
repercussions of a hymn to
death in variations of an unearthed
happiness in lieu of rondo
when the circle was smashed by the hymn
(no one deserves better to leave
that model of a house) where you say
I will be kept crucially updated
but the undated "soul" held together

as if by black hinges or
murdered city's black snow I cannot see
But I see the pages of your books
opening wildly like the unfinished tulips
the excess and potlatch of the sun
Return, return to me
lost student of the plague

II. OLD POEMS

Sinking, below the star-several harps
of evening, in one distant garden,
the new poem, twisted from the skin of the old whining birch—
Perhaps I am also dedicated to an angel's memory
her long black hair collected in my bed.
Now the youngest poet cries. I love countdowns! I love
the last few seconds of joy!
But the old poet knows the error in transcription
is correct: Nirvana is some sorrow.
Remember our last hacked Ariels
lie ruined in their melody. Two poems, folded, twisted together.
The earliest song: Because you have joined me
this great tree was felled. Is it worthless?
Because you have joined
never to leave again
spring has become the spring I had hoped for
and this crooked pebble is singing in the forest.
But the new poem, the winter flower, is not sweet.

III. WILD PSALM

In another world, listening to a Yemenite dump
Dreaming of Jerusalem our popular flesh,
A sleeper a singer whose name is a triple pun
A language where skin would be light,
It all sounds like the king's first love.
But in this world we sit to translate.
God splits and the blind man's reference
Ends like the war ever not quite.
As we forget the grammar we are of red clay, an idiot.

The suppliants approach, on the field of untranslatable force.
Simone says nothing but: Poetry
More difficult than mathematics, as I warned you.
And the old poets, and the books appear themselves,
Holiness in Sin, that enraged Gershom—the doubled books
And the body's words: Blessed is He who created the creation.
Blessed are they who created the blessing.

IV. THE WEAK POET

for Michal Govrin

When a poet is weak,
like a broken microphone,
he still has some power,
indicated by a red light.

The weak poet
is fixed to the wall
like an ordinary light.

Dependent and dismal by turns,
he is a nominalist
and a razor blade
and a light

And the demons cry,
Cast him from the kingdom
for a copy of a copy!

Remove him
like the women who supported the temple-
slaves too free and alive.
His similes are ingenious, like science among lovers.

My friend, however early
you called, you had come
too late, again.

The weak poet
has not gone grey
but his sacrificed similes
lead nowhere.

And his I is like any other word
in the newspaper and he is cut up
like fashion.

Each window was seductive,
but even his diseases could be cured.
Your low voice alone
is major like a skepticism.

We had forgotten
the place and the stories,
and the fiery method, too familiar, too distant.

We had memorized the poems,
but only for prison.
With the first new year celebrated in chaos
above the red waters of Paradise.

Where a clayey groom
hears the bride's voice
like a stronger world—

Sound is all
a snake can do—
and charming sense
and strangeness

Now the old poet
loses his voice like a garden.
But finds it again, like a street in a garden.

In the injured house
made of local sun and stone—
In the city of numbers
which everyone counts and hates and wants—

We could read together in a dark city garden,
scribbling with language over
screens like lips, scribbling the first mistranslations.

V. THE POEM WITH A FOOTNOTE

Who but he
Would talk to a teapot
She deposed in a dream
Who but he

But that's what a poet I replied
Does His occupation Rosemarie
He talks to a teapot
And a teapot talks back to him

What do you think writing unity
Is The poet is never alone
Talking at night to a teapot
The teapot talks back to him

He wrote six-foot poems
She received the letters
And put them in order ceaselessly
But how do we know the order

In which he received them (him) for real
Out of time like out of stamps
Torn time so funny so unfunny like a zebra
Kicking and almost killing you my mother

The poet takes a day off*
Never to work with the glass tower master
No more than he hears birds in his sleep
An ordinary goose goes squawking across the parking lot

The poet is photographed like a baby in a womb
The poet talks but not alone to the teapot
And it all sings (back to him)
It the your you speaks back to him

O simple world
It talks back to him
Even a goose though common
In time

Though aggressive and fat
In New Jersey
Beautifully bends its neck
In fog to speak

*He works and you work and I
There is only one day off
There is no day off
For a bug in a forest.   Recommence

The footnote hangs
Like a hair in space
Hair that became over time
A blue dolphin

VI. VOICELESS

They were right who inveighed against
the voice,
too sexual an organ
the rabbis those laryngologists
those who stopped a doctor
by their side like a singer
who refused to listen
and put a wall where voice had been
                          they died the lover of branches
of fire of the tape recorder used for good or ill your burning hair

If we were blind
and if we were known to listen
we would find one another
by your voice alone
(what you loved or Lilith loved was you and yes and permission)
and we are blind

VII. LIGHT BULB

1960

Our father
restless afraid of death
would say You will rest
when you're dead

Perhaps not!
And: Practice or you'll eat
in the garage
with the dog

Dead as the light
bulb is living still
A secret for the light bulb
is the nap

of broken music
There are some veins
in brown plaster
But the world emits

a little light
You wore cereal boxes
as a belt
I wore electric light

as another mistake
The search continued
for more veins and
a dented skull

This too had a pedestal
or place
or base or double
door or triple tomb.

VIII. LONG LIVE THE SNOWFLAKE

Long live the instant
long live the king and queen
killers in their vaccary
Long live
the tour around the periplus
with walkie-talkies in a drift
Long live a city by a destroyed lake
and simple water-clocks
Long live the word dark
the poet who was once a whiz
and a concert-master
art historian of
dhurries desperately and is now
just a poet

Long live the double foyer
of your undestroyed body
and our bed made out of the oaken earth
Long live such displacements
as are possible in the skena
of lack of recognition
Long live the unweaving
Long live the pierced son
Long live the middle-aged
sagging home from oblivion
to other caves
Long live the catachresis
of our lives in New Jersey
and Troy and in wandering eraser fluid
and books of many naked devices
Long live the interruption
of this fragile art

And long live it
when the sun beats
on a living shelter
and clarifies each blade
and the heavenly breasts
stand out to be sucked
and the earth bursts

IX. SONG FOR HANNAH ARENDT

Out of being torn apart
comes art.

Out of being split in two
comes me and you. HA HA!

Out of being torn in three
comes a logical poetry. (She laughed but not at poetry.)

Out of the essential mistranslation
emerges an illegitimate nation.

Better she said the enraged
than the impotent slave sunk in the Bay.

Out of being split into thirteen parts
comes the eccentric knowledge of "hearts."

(Out of being torn at all
comes the poor-rich rhyme of not knowing, after all.)

And out of this war, of having fought
comes thinking, comes thought.

X. UTTER AVENUE

He deduced from all aesthetics
in small boldface with shining serifs:
"He got nothing"
Translated from the Norwegian:
"Pleasure is so difficult,
like tennis, like music,
sorrow is so sly, so easy."
He wept all over the dream.
Received the dream-letter:
"Forgive me for (you) using you
It jolts me to think of uh it—"
Theology had apologized.
At the old grammar school, at the beginning,

father exploded. A critic wrote
"I'm not much on textures,
dreams, verbal links;
and not very big on satire, either."
Thank you for liking the last line the subject on fire
        or fire in the photograph.

XI. PRAYER FOR A HOUSE

Blessed is the architect of the removed structures
Blessed is the structure that weathers in spring snow like lies
Blessed is the crystal that leaps out of the matrix like a fool
And blessed is the school

Blessed factures
Blessed like spring snow
Blessed like a fool
And burnt book

Is the school a structure or weather
Or a lie like spring snow
And is the matrix leaping also like a fool
And is the book built or burnt?

Blessed is the removed
Blessed too the inlay like spring
Blessed is the tiger of the matrix like a found fool
And blessed the unbuilt like a book

Blessed is the architect who survives all removal
Blessed is the trapped structure like a gift
Blessed is the crystal fool
And blessed is the school

Blessed is the cut and the cry
Blessed the body of the patient in spring snow like lies
Blessed is the crystal stepping out of the matrix like a fool
And blessed is a burning book

Blessed is the anchorite and the architect in the dark smudge
Blessed is the remover bending to remove

Blessed is the folly leaping out of matrix
And blessed is the empty center

Blessed burning structures
Blessed like snowy spring
Blessed cry blessed in the matrix like a cut fool
And blessed each unlit book

Blessed is the architect of the removed cut
Blessed the structures that weather in lies like spring snow
Blessed is the crystal that leaps out of the matrix like a fool
And blessed is the school, like a burning library

Old new prayer
Old new song
Blessed is the crystal and the cry and the matrix like a painting fool
And blessed is the school

Song of the Eiffel Tower

for Lillian and Meyer Schapiro

Before the Eiffel was complete
Seurat painted it like a street
The top was a cloud, the skin was a dot
And like a nude the whole was in doubt.

The sky had no electric bulb.
But the sky was an electric bulb
For those who saw it clearly with a frame
And rented a window, but without a name.

And Meyer Schapiro
saw it all
In Conte crayons in the
caricatural fall.
The woman who posed was
a tower too.
Long before the
drawing drew.

And Daniel Shapiro
went to the deYoung
When he too
could hardly be called young.
He saw the Eiffel
in red and blue
In a deep case
without a postcard
view.

Drew my attention
to the small nude
of the Eiffel Tower
in its mad wood.
Like a bird in
the froth,
like a fish
in the flood.

Like a medieval
song transposed
by the mind.

We've lost it
again, like
Greek monody.
All we have is
a somber xerox copy.

Oh Eiffel Tower
Oh Sonia Delaunay
with elephantiasis
unto our day.
Let the stet stand,
let the series be
as lengthy as the
speckled tower
And all the rest
is money.
In that century,
we will be
happily blind.

Standing in such an iridescent wind.

The Eiffel
was nothing but numbers
like a lecture
by Plato
Now you may misspell
misspelling
Now you may hold your
organ like the
hero Balzac
Now you may be accused
of renting only
a house that opens

opens onto the Eiffel
and a dog on a
leash that explodes
into a light bulb

Crack open
the street,
break the
concrete.
It is distance,
it is near.
Only the junk
of the day remains,
only the top of the
peak, the poetics
of engineering
you will never reach
in everyday life:
our school.
In the picnic
on the peak,
a bridge away from
the disappearing mystique.
Oh and the lower
corner bears water
like Brooklyn,
the blue sky's name.

And a dark Lethe no doubt a copy
Ran like an academic stream filled with candy.
His father was the one-armed bailiff.
But the Tower was as strong as a shell-fish.

Desire Lines

I can see
  I cannot see
Keats in surgery in the 19th century
I can see
I cannot see
Mars and Aphrodite
dancing in the net
while the gods played and laughed at
                  the castanet
I can see
I cannot see
Keats and Fanny
Allen Ginsberg in 1953
I can see
I cannot see
    An adult
      Is a raindrop
    A raindrop
      Is an adult
I can see
I cannot see
  Lou Andreas Salome and
              Friedrich Nietzsche
Mars and Botticelli
Keats and Fanny B
Allen and Peter Orlovsky
Elizabeth and "and"

I can see
I cannot see
  An adult
   Is just an instrument
     A landscape pornography
     That hill is a hole
I walk on desire lines
You walk on desire
    I can see
    I cannot see

Dante and Beatrice
(At Forty-Seven)

are kitsch six inches of a gold bronze toy
sculpture on my wife's dead grandmother's
delicate end-tables ours
separated by a red grave and pink
candles and some smaller
horribly-shaped vegetable-like candles pointing
Dante looks like the mayor showing not pointing
of a small-town corruption
in a small cap he wears not against the
winter a cruel righteous careerist
grim as glucose and morose to boot
boasting of pride like a tiger on a street
Beatrice in nightgown her sin hope
a girl always about to go to bed
by herself and her long ringlets
as voluptuous as her nightgown
She is sexual and sad and refuses
to look at that business-man of words
all this a gift from Mickey Mouse who
said when he saw them it had to be
for me Goofy who took the sleep
out of the Comedy and took the
flowers and took the fathers, too
until what was left for a fatuous cento
like a student who translates
all vulgarity into ancient Greek a mistake

So if a person loves you they could say
I want to be in Hell with you forever
like two bats summoned on a windy
word by a poet having a mid-life decision
Both are ready for bed after six centuries
of poetry and epic youth and new songs
but I don't think they will do much
in bitter Riverdale like intense butterflies
She's perhaps too much the mother of Christ

and he's had a bad day in exile's
office writing to Miss Stone a stone himself in grass
He has a vague memory of this golden
sister her beginning breasts like end-words

But his mind is intent on astronomical
details like halakhic investigations
She turns out to be my melancholy mother
hoping working for better schools for
black children in South Africa
and justice like a child's story
This is a monstrous mixed marriage
and should be put an end to like a too-
accompanied sonata and before a dream
he's a generation too old and she
should indeed sleep with Romeo/Marat dying
in her glorious lap like a bronze invasion
He is the terror of the old last poet alive

diplomat of letters and lives
plunging the real prayer into the unreal earth
And I in love with each word and her wordlessness
Her shadow on the white world down the wall
God is a candle

After Three Chinese Poems

for Mr. Cong

One word tied to another word—that is all
You know. No cherry blossoms. In this world
The hospice workers visit the dead child.
His lack of a voice startles the sleeping words.

This world, fold upon fold.
Is there a better title for it?
Letting Go, Griefwork, Brightness Falls from the Air,
All the Angels Were There. She said it.

All night I think about my sister.
Galileo plunged into Jupiter.
O clear poetry!
No dust tonight.

Tall Rock In the Form
of an Old Child

to Richard Rosenblum

A man hid himself
and lived in a thin rock.
The king heard his name
and desired a sick visit.
But the old man was outside
and would not come inside.
The king screamed Old man, weak poet
visit me—The old child
replied: You visit me,
weak king. A student
is better than a president
The king could only agree
and offered him a job. Or cut his neck.
The old man said: This jade is a joke, it
splits and famous rich men
who take government positions
lack unity. I am going
home backwards and hide
in a secret day: the old way.
He grew up inside a rock
and never strayed from that
thin and watery rock. Today
the knife mark is on our neck. Holes.

Thin, because a student's scrawny.
Wrinkled, like your damaged face.
Holes, because our clothes are finished.
(Architecture is drunk like mud.)
The house of water hides itself.

Bambino Ebreo

(Daniel sleeping)

If I could only look
without ceasing
distortion of Thessalonians
I keep looking as into
soft plaster   golden sculpture
or weak bronze   or melting charcoal
and your lack of dreams
pierces me like a dream
You are growing up
in the lap of the gods
and I the mistranslator
stare at you like a student
unable to trace your
shadow as you dismiss it
with a swipe of crayons
unable even to photograph
your shadow
like the Akan parent
someone wants you in their
luxurious bed with designs
But you are mine
Someone wants to teach you
the proper way to make an S
and upside down A's would become
habitable horrors
But you are mine

Someone wants to teach you names
in a family of rules
But you are mine

Christ in Prague

Christ collects his own blood
In a rudimentary chalice
Outlined by a childish master
His skin is grey like patched-up plaster
The angels who surround us are young
Their wings are fish
And buckles around their neck
With keyholes to the gate
Brown blood keeps falling from his nailed head
Panicked and sad, another victim
Black blood keeps falling from one hand like paint
And red blood from his beard
Like crayon blotches
The blood is the color after all of his
        excellent long hair
It falls like tears from the crown of thorns
When the blood reaches the cup it turns golden
And the gold sun behind him shines with triple colors

I Loved You Once by Pushkin

I wish I had a copy
of Pushkin's poem
"I loved you once"
which is said to achieve
the intended effect—
"wistful resignation
half-concealing half-
revealing a still
smoldering passion"
"without having recourse
to figures of speech."
O it would be clear to you then
there could be such a thing—
I would leave you a copy.

On a Tennis Court

Playing without a net's
not such a bad idea.
And what if the
Emperor's clothes
were a good idea,
as the painter said to me.
Playing tennis in the dark:
a lot like poetry.
Playing tennis in
autumn leaves, is that
too much like poetry.
Tennis is a game,
therefore not poetry.
Nor is it a dream,
the opposite of stupidity.
But it is "the
articulatory dance of the speech-
organs." You play it
in a field, the visual
field without an eye.
You play it against a wall,
it rebounds endlessly.
By day, you are a tennis player.
By night, the famous other awakes
to brass and violins
that white-out you and me.
The friends disperse.
You engrave the tennis
court, enmeshed like bottles.

The net flaps, like
a melancholy faith.
Only the businessman
is confident, like an
old metre, lilting.
Playing tennis without
a net's not such a poor idea.
Playing tennis in the
dark is a lot like poetry.

A Found Golf Ball

Part of the universe has been found   But only part!
but it is the light of dead stars
if it shall console you
and the light of our own dying sun
and it is the light of dark matter
along the edges of our time like the exhausted flesh of a single flower
though it could be "something else," normal and glowing
like your mother's voice
where you hoped to find another voice
and my father's name
which bore no middle initial
so he gave me a middle initial
so I would not write in time of war
No Middle Initial
Part of the universe has been found   Only a part!

Do you take the part for the whole I asked you
and you said I take the part for the part
and the missing woman sang around the edges
We do not know what the body can do
and the painter said You will die
like a poisoned nude reaching for the telephone
And the longer the brightness lasts, the more massive the intervening dark
It is not our custom to pray in the direction of the Tower of Babel
And it's all ordinary, the stars, the stuff of love, and the dark found universe

Found Time

Lost like the beautiful slave
who trembled imprecisely
at the poem
a slave to thought or painting or
thief with a stolen book on crime
The conversation held a history of appalling jokes
on lost familial conversation
in horrified presentiment
That is the fountain I will not build
with a concrete line carved for a dream
a galaxy glimpsed
As scientistic oddity tiny light too late
Sunken in hypnotic purity the too-human
receives a bullet in the wrist
Later knows he has lost the marvelous, finally mis-
translated as a radiant wrong

But let a cold materialism reign
in the time of the crone-beauty puzzle the face-vase the rabbit-and-duck
in bronze the shadow of a child
the second half and all our shadows
in bronze the unreadable X and gilded lily
the golden section golden architect must sleep
the victim and the sleepless spiral sleep together
And in hanging strips the novel of our lives
dripping with disaster
as we rush through the transparent constellations
stamped and folded with a terrifying anecdote growing downwards
walking on the carpet of black wings
a carpet of language in shreds also with a copy of
that starry albatross now just wings
voiceless like a skull in the shape of broken words
in the time of found objects found shadows found time

The Car in a Maze

with Daniel

I believe the world is like a maze
When you make a wrong turn
It's like making a mistake in a maze
Cars make a lot of mistakes
Angels ride along with their little xylophones
God stays where he is
Cars can get bumped into leaves
Angels sleep for the whole day
God stays where he is
The moon hates to go in front of the sun
The sun hates to go in front of the moon
I don't like to get lost in the maze you have to walk in
Angels like to get lost in God—God is never lost
I like to get lost in my house

In Memory of Goofy

All the characters are dying, Donald Duck,
And not just Superboy in competition
An international competition for the grave
Of Goofy's going up
And everyone is guilty of perspective
But what's perspective now when Minnie's ill
A hole in her lungs and tumor on her heart
And Goofy tried hypnosis for his pain
In the end all neon lights in Gotham have gone grey
With pain. And the frogs keep disappearing like receding lines
And we grow rare as frogs.

Will they sue us, Huey cries to Louie hoarsely,
Because we are all skewered on the ropes like pipes again
But we were born for sculpture like adventure
And Uncle Scrooge keeps diving in his pool of money
Mostly to find an image—
Not of himself but of one poor water-poisoned frog.

It's a grid system Dewey sighed to Louie,
And the flecks of paint or crayon both remind us
We are all condemned, like little words beneath eraser fluid.
Don't know whether we are rushing towards
The island of love or leaving it, as always.
More slowly some improve but most are not reviving
Not even for some sequel in the stores.
Now Goofy's gone and all his five-act plays
His stories neatly typed, his wasted too-commercial years.
He was expert in light. Bad taste, bad taste just thinking,
Cried Jughead, but most for saying anything, after all.

Then Daniel in a T-shirt chirruped brightly

I like birds of prey and he liked songbirds
I like a raptor circling wildly
He liked a sparrow singing on a mirror.
But all the flightless birds are howling for a charm.
And the black window is draped in green for Goofy.
Return, return, lost student of the plague.

A Cross for Joseph

Of course,
Christ was a woman
On certain crosses:

Zealot, Essene, saboteur,
Husband, hypnotist:
Each joke is a scandalous coffin for a carpenter.

All relics
Of his penis triangular
Speak of those distant eyes:

Surviving all pigments,
All hypocrisies.
Dripping into geometrical cups

Like an antithetical glyph—
Peace, cleave, evening, goodbye—
An interior of the cross

Must be made!
Mannerist androgyne
With attenuated hands,

Accept a spike
For and against all kitsch.
This was an execution, after all.

The political locks
Dangle down. A crown
Is just the rose tried upside down.

Subversion, inversion, perversion:
Beneath him, all perspective now:
Hovels and happiness of the very poor

Always with you: constancy
Of the homeless.
Oh what shall I carve for you, heteronymic madman?

A pig before pearls
A camel caught by a rabid needle
A dead son burying his living father?

Your other plain or silver stories—
Popular at last, you hang
With your triumphant narrative

While we waver below—
With your family, like a tradition
Without philosophers—

In this desert of a skull,
The thunder makes us tremble
Like new dogs

Because it seems as if a tremendous dog
Waves judgment days above us
From a multiple sick jaw.

There is a small slit
Through which your mother
Can see you still.

Mary With Sleeping Child

Our mother is always awake
and her baby is always asleep
Are they both wrapped in gold after all
Or is it just paint: a veil

She is ordinary in ordinary mourning
and her baby is not going to live
She leans her curls against his skull
because she is awake but he is thought

Her big hands were cut by stone-cutters
when the world was rich and brown
Her eyes are tired because he is an old man
a little corpse in ghostly swaddling

You say it is all for the love of a child
but she would like to sob with her beautiful neck
and her ornamental uneconomical curls
the beautiful that could not save this child

At the foot of the Cross
that has grown within her
She will remember his loud rebuke
and infinitesimal fingers curled together without end

The historians have applied the X-rays
and they found nothing
They were searching for gold and haloes and dates
She was offering the ordinary meal again

She is awake and in trouble and he is dreaming
of riots, earthquakes, cut flesh, fire, open graves
and a lion on its discontented path
and his blood dripping into his mother's cup

Our mother's eyes are open but he has turned away
in a dream of cities and palms, victories
that looks like catastrophe, and indestructible fury
and silence which he will maintain his whole life

And silence in which he will maintain our life

A Song for Rudy Burckhardt

And so the snow fell
And covered up poetry.

And so the snow fell
And covered up cities like bags of leaves.

And so the snow fell
And covered up an architecture.

And so the snow fell
And covered one red orange sexual flower.

And so the snow fell
And covered the bus and the passengers.

And so the snow fell
And covered up our friend.

And so the snow fell
And covered his clear water-towers, his windows and his door.

And so the snow fell
And covered up the word poetry.

And so the snow fell
And covered up the snow and a house within.

And so the snow fell
And fell on his fallen trees.

And oh the snow fell
And covered up his photographs of snow.

And so the snow fell
And covered up even passing clouds.

For the Evening Land

"What causes a death rattle?"—*The New York Times*

If there is a sound before death in America
What causes that sound
Asks the newspaper
For most there is no sound
Only a dream of two words: White black
Irreversible or the dream without words
There is no voice in America
Only the finite
Reading the voices
But let me die singing, like the forefathers
Lightning never hits the obtrusive pole.
But the animals shrivel in the field.
And the obscure observer takes a note.
And what is that sound before death—
They have banished the death rattle, the rhonci, the rales.
We die elsewhere, of something else.
And what is that last sound my mother made
Softly made: archaic breathing. And do not call it a dream.
Nor is it a game: The child says infinity is a small word
We have done away with noise and have left only
The agonal respiration like war material.
You will paint the Americans but is it
The father in a grain of dust, heroic androgyne with honeysuckle
Man in a skirt, woman in a flower, faithless but free
The child thinks the god's birthday must be every day:
He is that old. Fool's gold folly. Crystals slouch out of matrix.
While the spider illuminates his influence with a film
Of joy, the fly develops his refuge in a shattered theme
The dead sunflower almost blocks the sun
Like an old poet, an empty eye coerces us
Like an old fate, the gods are dipped in water and predict
Man is red dust, let there be flesh.
There is no sound before death in America
You do not see the charred soldier, only pleasure.
We have done away with all noise, but the agony of respiration.
And autumn will be the flag of that new nation.

Winter Work

A dog prays.
    For me.
He barks inside all day, what little inside there is, like a pigeon.
Help!
He kneels for his king one night
Kind owner. "Ayekah?" All is kind,
    All is cruel.
A dog's prayed, obeyed, spayed.
In the forest now, he moans for help
In some of his languages. No one!
The addressee slips away,
Has slipped away.
But a dog thinks.
The dog thanks you in the desert.
In the desert
Of the desert, you have left a trace.

After Poetry

"I want my son to grow powerful and rich through science."
—RIMBAUD

Now that I have given up poetry,
The guest of poetry,
Governed poetry,
Or rather that poetry has given up me,
Has queened my pawn, how green my pawn,
Or rather that poetry died in my lap,
Any lap, like a lousy lover
In another language, and I
A Luddite with a laptop in his lap

And now that my son is subtle
And malicious as a god, any god,
And bestrides the dogmatic world
As if it were a tennis court

The clouds pass by, almost inhuman
Like passers-by, the mountains like
Churches and the churches like mountains
Beautiful and untranslatable a woman
Walks past the park like a street
Or a scream or a double and triple
Loss of meaning, and I thank whatever
Nothing we actually worship, to change
Nothing and the important thing: to leave
The world alone, largely uninterpreted
For the wet pavement
On which he may scratch his poems

Weequahic Park in the Dark

J. Ceravolo died 1988

Oh Joe
We walked across the lake
"That's no way to walk"
You loved each bug and the cosmos
But you had no job
Oh Joe
It was an Olmstead almost
With ducks and a track
And a temple on top
Women washed their cars
And you loved the baby
Under lacy incubation
With your engineer's respect
Oh Joe

Allen Ginsberg walked beside me
Confessed his visions might not be real
But I had seen God in dungarees
In daylight in the waves at Deal
Predict the destruction of the bulwark
Weequahic Park in the dark
And you had read the conscious lake
Oh Joe full of the dignity of the seasons your school

You explained—
I see the words around the emotion
Then I write them down—
It was your system of the spider-web
You were sad
But couldn't explain

Missing you now like an oak in 1962
Or the word oak
I see your spider-web I write it down
Open to me, Weequahic Park

Where the shadow of a cloud passed over
As I lay on my back in the sunny court
As I lay on the lake in the boat
Thinking I could never die

In a Fold

for Jeremy Gilbert-Rolfe

the fog eats the bridge
the George Washington
is for a moment occluded
God does not exist
just six emerald lights
The diver disappears
the string hangs precisely
the hand says hello help and goodbye
Then he swims away strongly

Homeless man in a yellow jacket
arranges his orange bed
Commuters do not bother him
pitiless as Spinoza he dozes on the ramp

for a moment God does not exist
the bridge does its yoga sturdily
not exactly affirmative
an opaque pigeon slides through
the bridge is a temporary shelter a sukkah
the skull that laughs
naked unclad these fifty years
a necklace at night
but in the white mild morning
at the end of endings

near three Nervi stockades of
a bus terminal I wait
the chlorophyll's loss astonishes you
the baroque drapery of the fog
an abstraction to delete repose

No Explosives is a sign
like woman or large vehicles
yourself a temporary shelter
theme of refuge

For a moment the bridge disappears
house above the river
without whimsy or parody
I remember my first fearful walk across
but now only immense demography
Last week three earnest pedestrians
came towards me with guns
to arrest my neighbor
he meekly submitted I sidled off
to denounce him or simply look
as that submissive one surrounded
by jubilant plainclothes—
The next day someone smashed him from the air

A bridge is a dangerous
neighborhood City birds know that
In a fold in a white moderate morning at the end of endings

NEW POEMS
(2 0 0 7)

Don Quixote, Reading

Today I
didn't know
whether
I was Don
Quixote,
reading
about Don
Quixote,
and getting
angry,
or Sancho
Panza
dreaming
he really is
Sancho
Panza
moaning in
the
greyblue
distance
as if he had
"turned
 into" Don
Quixote
and when I
entered my
casement
window
I didn't
know
whether I
was David
reading in
the dark
or writing in
the dark,
whether a
white

butterfly
could be my
father
returning to
the branch,
to the walk
around the park,
or poetry
which
cannot be
an optical
illusion, as
a critic
of illusions
once put it
wrongly.
As for
Dulcinea, I
am so
impressed
that she
never
appears
except
 like any
wave.
I know,
I do not
know
whether I
am fat and

short and
ugly
D Sancho
Panza or a
good

governor
with political-
theological
ideas,
or the lean
Don
besmirched
by another
Don,
wearing
cardboard
for part of a
hat
when my
own Master said
it should be
gold, gold
all the way
through
though most poetry
is
pyrite,
and we love
a dream of
inexpensive
materials.
like earth.
And so I sit
like a
collector
or a clown
or a dead
mule. A
hanged man
in the
distance,
another

David cries
out for me
to stop it.
But you are
more beautiful
than any bag,
as beautiful
as the direct
sentence
You are
the hidden
fire and a concealed knife.

Colorful Hands

I put hands on your feet—a green hand
A yellow hand near your knee—colorful hands
I put a purple hand near your neck
And a green and light green hand on your spine

In the air beyond your bed, an orange hand
To the right of your night table a dark hand
I put an outstretched purple hand over your hair
A red hand on your hip says Goodbye, evening, enemy.

One red hand could cover you. I placed a guitar on your upper lip
And a trumpet. And between your lips a conductor's baton
And on your lower lip two violin bows and a red banjo, silent.

And on your pattern I placed more music.
And on your breast, nothing.
In the sky, I placed a bridge of violets held up by no string.

Hapax Legomena

I covered you and cover you
I colour you and uncover you
My dream intent to discover you seems clear

as a snowflake dresses you and undresses you
an orange hand upon your breast unless it's you
a purple simple hand on your hand is less than
you

you covered and recovered you
Drinking water
   Sampling station

A Polaroid at night of trees on fire:
words written only once—
words used only once—

your naked face the origin of the world—

You spit into the ocean
and make it sweet for me

A Riverdale Address

Now I am engaged
in a great civil war
testing—whether my "I"
or any "I" can long endure.
(Love is a Battlefield by
Pat Benatar) We have met
on a portion of that self
to dedicate a poor ion It is not fitting
or filling or proper,
but "we" did it.
In a smaller sense, we
cannot be delicate or renovate
the hollow self. The
living dead—Meyer S
Fairfield Porter Kenneth
John H—have dedicated
it far below our poor
potency to flow or subtract
to carve assemble or let be.
It is rather for us
(I is a pronoun or
shifty shifter) the dead living
(The world forms
two straight lines
as is said on the street)
to be consolidated
to that immeasurable scale
And that without bigness
we take from their greatness
a complete devotion
to one note that in them
we live and vainly die
And that the poetry
of earth is as good
as the poetry of language
And that poetry of
the self by the self and for

the self will perish
from the earth and
that the poetry of the
earth without contempt
for an apple (The whole tree
repeats the leaf)
will not perish, like the earth.

The Foot Speaks

Each thing speaks and seems monolingual:
The dead flowers try their silent Esperanto
The squirrel squeaks and begs:
Without poverty, there are no words.
A tree would rather dance but declines
The bush shuts up.
The hedge is an expressionist.

Each car has its own idiolect.
The street uses English, even.
Each door aims to be clearer.
The summer window suffers emphysema
And coughs during discussions of Cressyd.

Yes your blue obsessive jay imitates consciously.
Quoth the raven: I am language.
I am language,
And nothing in language is strange, to me.

Song for an Envelope

If I were
your patient
And You were my
healer
All day you would
heal me
And I would be patient

You tease me Don't
worry
My act could be fetching
You'd cook me quinoa
And I would eat slowly

Together we'd live
reduced
in a shoe made of
plaster blessings

in a wall house of

rammed earth
in Holland
watery subway

I'd teach you the
cloudy chords
You'd sing
the empty words
Full tigers would calm us
You'd hypnotize the tides

For you the horizon lies
For you green seaglass shines
As a child loves turquoise
shameless songs
end surprisingly

We would heal finally
Fold screens and scientific
fruit
You'd heal me with your hair
your harp
I'd be our first patient always

All day my lucky wounds
would heal
in your bandages
of blue sea algae
Your solar mill would sigh like smoke
our City melt in the friendly sun

You'd offer me those
useless herbs
I'd analyze
even Paradise
You'd heal me
with water not poison
my medicine would be
a cheap accordion

Little Low Tech

The only palm presentation I will make
will be reading your palms one day
for long life lines on the field of battle
and intricate love lines and laugh lines
on the field of your face.

Song for Another Envelope

The fatal exceptions occurred
without exception and not fatally.
They stole my throne from me:
it was a tree, or a tree
stump as they rotted it,
cut it to a chair,
as democratic as a T
then sank it into the ground
and I forgot to take last snaps
of a serious mossy thing.
Fire at evening, or was it the
evening on fire?

Reader,
butterfly,
migrant drunk, ally,
unemployed luminosity,
minnow, in the air, feather,
scrawny light—
You decide.

After Ryokan

In my cup

In the thin snow

In front of your window
In the window sky
In the blue distance
In the scattered doors

In the pool near your room
In the shadow on the highway
In every quarter of the evening land
In the staves of the sky

I seem to hear your voice

Subject: A Song

> Out of the crooked timber of humanity,
> no straight thing was ever made.
>
> —Kant

Out of the pills and the pencils, out of toothbrushes and night guards, out of CD's and Altoids, out of feathers and staplers, out of time clocks and syllabi, out of tissues and scissors, nothing straight has ever been made.

Out of computers and mousepads, out of CD's and CD ROMS, out of pens and sedentary mentalisms, out of philosophers and lampshades, out of pennies and a penis, out of calculators and prescription pills, out of envelopes and white envelopes, out of industrial shelving and the moonlight, nothing straight has ever been made.

Out of Venetian blinds and dream-catchers, out of dreams of Lichtenberg and the desire of art history, out of war and branches, out of shadows of my fingers and your hand, out of your riveting nipples and her weightless eyes, out of rockets and buttons, out of the number 5 and out of a red rhino, out of mustaches and Mona Lisas, out of black numbers, nothing straight has ever been made.

Out of colored sand and autumnal trophies, out of chaos and beds, out of a crooked woman and the straight edge of a crystal, out of jade and dust, out of mankind's poor penis and the archaic song of sacrifice, out of Pluto, Medea, and Goofy, out of black boots and Van Gogh's shoes, out of a battered self-portraiture, nothing straight has ever been made.

Out of baseballs and dresser drawers, out of blue jays and imitation, out of snow inside worlds and the universe in a walnut, out of no place and the best place, out of an image of hope and the abjection of jargon, out of sheaths and blossoming antennae, on the day without adjectives, out of the absolutely necessary meeting of the girl and the swan, bestial for the swan, nothing entirely straight has ever been made.

Out of words, out of dictionaries and guesses, out of the contingent letter and the space between letters, out of the tongue and the T, nothing straight has ever been "built."

Out of the forest that somewhat covers me, out of the desire and the strangled globe, out of the forced marriage of the feather the pen and the eraser fluid, out of shadows of light, out of the almost invisible sheath and the dream of tactility, out of the swan and the sign, out of the dream and the game and the impossible, on the day of the permanent flaw, with the heat of it, nothing entirely straight was ever made.